Donated
By

Delaware
County
Hall of Fame

"There's no doubt in my mind that Mickey Vernon has Hall of Fame credentials. Without question, he belongs." – **PHILLIES HALL OF FAME BROADCASTER HARRY KALAS**

"He was a role model for me. I saw how a guy from Marcus Hook could make it." – **FORMER PRO FOOTBALL STAR BILLY (WHITE SHOES) JOHNSON**

"He was one of the best first basemen I ever played with or against. He was a wonderful ballplayer." – **FORMER SENATORS THIRD BASEMAN EDDIE YOST**

"I enjoyed every minute I had working with him. He was as pleasant as anybody I worked with. A gentleman. Very dignified. A real professional." – **ATLANTA BRAVES VICE PRESIDENT AND GENERAL MANAGER JOHN SCHUERHOLZ.**

———— QUOTES FROM LONG AGO ————

"He makes that worn-out phrase brand new: a credit to the game." – **BOB ADDIE IN *THE WASHINGTON POST***

"If I was pitching and it was the ninth inning and we had a two-run lead with the bases loaded and Mickey Vernon was up, I'd walk him and pitch to the next man." – **HALL OF FAME PITCHER SATCHEL PAIGE**

"I wouldn't mind having nine Mickey Vernons in the starting lineup." – **WASHINGTON SENATORS MANAGER BUCKY HARRIS**

"Mickey is the only man I know of in baseball who could play first base in a tuxedo, appear perfectly comfortable, and never wrinkle his suit." – **BALTIMORE ORIOLES ASSISTANT GENERAL MANAGER JACK DUNN**

"Mickey Vernon lives the kind of life on and off the ball diamond that is worthy of emulation by all the baseball young fry in the country." – ***CHESTER TIMES* EDITORIAL**

OTHER BOOKS BY RICH WESTCOTT

The Phillies Encyclopedia
(with Frank Bilovsky)

Diamond Greats

The New Phillies Encyclopedia
(with Frank Bilovsky)

Phillies '93 – An Incredible Season

Philadelphia's Old Ballparks

Mike Schmidt

Masters of the Diamond

No-Hitters – The 225 Games, 1893-1999
(with Allen Lewis)

Splendor on the Diamond

Great Home Runs of the 20th Century

A Century of Philadelphia Sports

Winningest Pitchers — Baseball's 300-Game Winners

Tales from the Phillies Dugout

*Native Sons – Philadelphia-area Baseball Players
Who Made the Major Leagues*

The Phillies Encyclopedia - Third Edition
(with Frank Bilovsky)

Veterans Stadium – Field of Memories

MICKEY VERNON

The Gentleman
First Baseman

BY
RICH WESTCOTT

FOREWORD BY AL ROSEN

Camino Books, Inc.
Philadelphia

Manufactured in the United States of America

1 2 3 4 5 08 07 06 05

Library of Congress Cataloging-in-Publication Data

Westcott, Rich.
  Mickey Vernon : the gentleman first baseman / by Rich Westcott.
    p. cm.
  ISBN 0-940159-94-5 (alk. paper)
  1. Vernon, Mickey, 1918- 2. Baseball players--United States--Biography.
I. Title.

  GV865.V46W47 2005
  796.357'092--dc22   2005007401

Cover and interior design: Jan Greenberg

This book is available at a special discount on bulk purchases for
promotional, business, and educational use.

Publisher
Camino Books, Inc.
P.O. Box 59026
Philadelphia, PA 19102

www.caminobooks.com

In memory of
Elizabeth (Lib) Firth Vernon

October 16, 1918 – December 17, 2004

CONTENTS

Foreword

At long last, there is a book about Mickey Vernon. A great baseball player. Yes. And a gentleman of the highest order with no peer as a friend.

Our relationship had a brief beginning, but it was nurtured and renewed in various ways over a period of six decades.

It started in 1944 during World War II. At military bases around the country, baseball was ever-present. There were teams throughout the Norfolk, Virginia, area. I was an aspiring 19-year-old Class D baseball player when I met a major leaguer. His name was Mickey Vernon.

The joy. The awe. And I had a life-long friend. I became his teammate, his opponent, and his boss. And I never met a finer man.

As a player, Vernon had grace, talent, and ability. The record books tell us of Mickey's numerical stats. But those of us who are blessed with his friendship will tell you of his soft-spoken wisdom, of his elegance, of his insight, of his deep conviction of right and wrong.

He was a player who could grace any lineup and have his teammates, manager, and coaches thrilled to be a part of that team.

His story is one that legends are made of. He is a legend to me—my friend. I just wish that he had gone 1-for-4 instead of 2-for-4 in the season's finale in 1953.

—Al Rosen

Acknowledgments

Few books—if any—are solely the work of just an author. In most cases, many people contribute to a published work, participating in the effort in a variety of different ways. So it was with this book. Many people pitched in. Without their help, writing a book of this kind would have been impossible. Accordingly, I wish to express my sincere appreciation to all of those who took an interest in this project and who went out of their way to help.

Foremost, of course, is the subject himself. Mickey Vernon made himself available for countless hours of interviewing, always exhibiting the highest level of patience, kindness, grace, and understanding. Just being with him for all those hours made the pursuit of this book an extremely worthwhile and extraordinary experience.

Thanks, too, to Mickey's daughter Gay Vernon for her invaluable help, support, and encouragement, and to Mickey's sister Edith Cushman for the wealth of information she provided.

I would also like to offer a heartfelt word of gratitude to Chubby Imburgia and Chuck Taylor, who were not only two of the earliest and staunchest supporters of this project, but whose help in so many other ways was truly immeasurable.

My gratitude extends to George Case Jr., Harry Chaykun, Joe Cirilli, Kit Crissey, Ed Gebhart, Bill Gilbert, Jim Hannan, Jim Hartley, Dick Heller, Joe McGillen, Ron Menchine, Tim Murtaugh, Russ Schneider, Louis Stesis, Russ White, and Matt Zabitka. I also offer a special thank you to Dave Smith of Retrosheet for once again providing extremely useful research material, to Herm Krabbenhoft for making available his and his colleagues' research on triple plays, and to publisher Edward Jutkowitz for his enthusiastic approach to this project and his foresight in seeing its merits as a book.

I thank Al Rosen, a most gracious gentleman who played several important roles in Vernon's career, for his touching foreword. I thank the dozens of people—family, friends, teammates, opponents, writers, broadcasters, and many others—who were good enough to share their opinions about Mickey and their experiences with him. And finally, I thank my wife Lois for her unyielding support and for sharing my enthusiasm for such an enjoyable mission.

Thank you everyone for your very special assistance.

Introduction

In the 1940s and until the mid-1950s, the premier first baseman in the American League was an extremely talented player who went by the name of Mickey Vernon. On a daily basis, no other first baseman could match his ability as both a hitter and a fielder.

His real name was James, but he had been called "Mickey" since he was three years old because of his fascination with a popular song of the same name.

"I would play the song over and over on the Victrola," Vernon recalled. "Eventually, one of my aunts started calling me Mickey. The name stuck, and I've been called that ever since."

By any name, Vernon was one of the marquee players in an era that many baseball authorities consider among the sport's finest. He won two batting championships, including one in 1946 when he outdistanced the fabled Ted Williams in a spectacular September stretch drive. His second title, won in 1953, was achieved when he edged Al Rosen in a torrid race that was finally decided on the last at-bat of the season.

Overall, Vernon hit .290 or above nine times, and finished his career with just under 2,500 hits. He was a member of seven American League All-Star teams.

"He is a high-voltage swatter," one report of the day gushed about Vernon's batting. Hall of Fame pitcher Bob Feller said that Mickey was one of the toughest batters he ever faced.

As good as he was with the bat, Vernon was just as good with the glove. No first baseman was ever more graceful around the bag. Mickey fielded his position as though he was engaged in a form of outdoor ballet. "He could play first base in a tuxedo," it was claimed. He led the first basemen of his league five times in fielding percentage. Even today, Vernon holds American League career records for first basemen for the most games played, chances, putouts, and assists, and he is the current major league record-holder for participating in the most double plays.

There is nothing unusual about getting to the ballpark early to watch batting practice, especially in this age of bulked-up hitters and easy home runs. But because of Vernon, coming to the ballpark early to watch—of all things—fielding practice was obligatory for admirers of his elegant style. Gliding around first base, the Washington Senators' W flapping on his chest for most of his career, Vernon elevated the practice of catching a baseball to the highest level of artistry.

Vernon is one of the few players to have performed in the major leagues in four decades. His major league career went from 1939 to 1960. Through most of that time, Mickey played with the Washington Senators. He also played with the Cleveland Indians, Boston Red Sox, Milwaukee Braves, and Pittsburgh Pirates. Bucky Harris, one of Vernon's managers, once said, "I wouldn't mind having nine Mickey Vernons in my starting lineup."

After retiring in 1960 as a player-coach with the Pittsburgh Pirates (winners of the World Series on Bill Mazeroski's dramatic walkoff home run in the seventh game) under his boyhood friend Danny Murtaugh, Vernon became the first manager of the expansion Washington Senators. Later, he was a coach with several other big league organizations, including the St. Louis Cardinals, Montreal Expos, Kansas City Royals, Los Angeles Dodgers, and New York Yankees, and a minor league manager, most notably in Vancouver and Richmond. Overall, Vernon's baseball career extended more than 50 years, ending as a scout in the 1980s with the Yankees.

Many baseball experts claim that Vernon "is the best first baseman not in the Hall of Fame." They're surely right. Indeed, there are first basemen now residing in the Hall of Fame with considerably lesser credentials than Vernon.

You would have gotten no argument about that from President Dwight D. Eisenhower. Ike not only marveled at Vernon's talent, Mickey was his favorite player. Once after Vernon had hit a game-winning home run, Eisenhower sent a Secret Service agent out onto the field to get Mickey and bring him over to his box for a special presidential congratulation.

Vernon was the favorite player of not just Ike. Among others who rank him at the top of their list are television host Maury Povich, Hall of Fame broadcaster Harry Kalas, and former baseball commissioner Bowie Kuhn. Kuhn and Povich grew up in Washington and as boys regarded Mickey as their favorite player. An unexpected but unforgettable experience with Vernon also made him Kalas' boyhood idol.

Few players were ever more popular than Vernon. Mickey was a favorite with both his teammates and opposing players and with legions of others, too. The fans of Washington adored him, treating him like royalty both on and off the field.

Mickey was one of the most popular players ever to pull on the uniform of the Washington Senators. In the minds of old Senator fans, he ranked right at the top with the storied Walter Johnson. When an all-time Washington team was chosen many years ago, Vernon was the team's first baseman, joining other luminaries such as Goose Goslin, Joe Cronin, Sam Rice, and Clyde Milan.

Nowhere, though, is Vernon regarded any higher than in his native Delaware County, the third heaviest-populated county in Pennsylvania and an area with a rich athletic tradition.

It can be said without the slightest amount of hesitation that Vernon is not only the best baseball player, but the most popular athlete ever to come out of the county. More than that, though, he is unquestionably one of the most revered people ever born in the county that sits in the southeastern corner of Pennsylvania. If Delaware County had a mayor, Mickey would have had a lifetime job.

There is a baseball league in Delaware County named after Mickey. He has been honored countless times by his fellow citizens, and he is still, years after his baseball days ended, a frequent subject of local newspaper articles and a regular on the banquet circuit. In 2003, Mickey's fans raised some $60,000 to erect a statue of him. The unveiling in Vernon's native Marcus Hook was so heavily attended that surrounding streets had to be blocked off.

In the early part of his career, Vernon had an interesting tour of duty during World War II, spending some of the time playing before thousands of troops in the South Pacific. While there, he befriended a young African American teenager named Larry Doby. The two became lifelong friends.

Making friends was another one of Vernon's strengths. He made scores of them. And he was recognized far and wide for his gentlemanly demeanor, his kind and considerate conduct, and his limitless good deeds. Vernon had the respect of all with whom he came into contact, and almost never did anyone have an unkind word to say about him.

Vernon is held in such high regard that when his former Washington roommate Walt Masterson was interviewed for this book, he asked the author if anyone had "said anything bad about Mickey." When told that no one had, Masterson said, "Well if anybody does, you send him to me, and I'll have a few choice words for him."

Such loyalty is typical not only of Mickey's teammates, but also of his opponents. When told about this project, the great Red Sox second baseman Bobby Doerr said, "You're writing about a very fine person. He is a class person, and I just can't say enough good things about him. He was tops."

Mickey Vernon is indeed "tops." And he has lived an enormously successful and interesting life. None have been bigger parts of that life than his late wife Lib, his daughter Gay, and his sister Edith, each of whom shares so many of Mickey's wonderful qualities.

For many years, I have wanted to write a book about Vernon. He was, after all, one of my boyhood idols, too. As a youngster, I clipped baseball pictures out of newspapers and magazines and pasted them into scrapbooks that, by the time I reached my teen years, formed a pile which, as I remember, must have been about three feet high. The first picture I ever clipped for that collection was of Mickey Vernon swinging a bat at Shibe Park. I still have that picture.

Many years went by, and then one fine day I actually met Mickey while assigned to do a newspaper article on him. Although I was just a cub reporter, I can't say that I was overwhelmed—or even a little scared. That's because Vernon is the kind of person who immediately puts people at ease. But I sure was thrilled.

Since that day some 40 years ago, I saw Mickey many times, sometimes writing about him, sometimes just talking, often at the ballpark where I covered games and Vernon scouted players. Such occasions were always highly pleasurable.

Now, at long last, the book about this stellar baseball player and gentleman has finally made it to press. Naturally, Vernon's special insights, stories, and accomplishments are important parts of the book. Just as important, though, are the comments by Mickey's baseball peers as well as his family and friends. Their stories about a man so universally admired are truly revealing.

It has been a special pleasure for me to have been able to write this book. And I hope that those who encounter these pages get as much enjoyment reading about the man as I did writing about him.

—Rich Westcott

A Model Citizen

Hall of Fame broadcaster Harry Kalas often tells the story of how he developed a love for baseball. It was all because of Mickey Vernon.

Kalas, the Phillies play-by-play man since 1971, was raised in Naperville, Illinois, a small town about 30 miles outside of Chicago. Let him provide the details:

"As a kid, I always liked baseball, and played on the sandlots. But I never had a chance to go out and see a Cubs or White Sox game," he said. "Finally, when I was 10 years old, my dad took me to my very first big league game to see the White Sox and Washington Senators at Comiskey Park. I was really excited.

"Because it was raining that day, there was only a very small crowd at the game. As a result, my dad was able to get seats right behind the Washington dugout.

"There was no batting practice because of the rain. So the players had nothing to do. Now, here's this wide-eyed kid—me—sitting behind the Senators dugout with my dad, taking it all in, and

1

some of the players came out into the dugout. Mickey Vernon was one of them.

"He popped his head out of the dugout, and saw me sitting there. Well, he reached over and picked me up, and took me into the dugout. He gave me a ball and introduced me to some of the other players. I was just in heaven. I was there for about 10 minutes, then he put me back in my seat.

"That really started my love for the game of baseball and the Washington Senators. I must have been the only one in the Chicago area who was a Senators fan. I remained one until they moved to Minnesota. My classmates always teased me about being a Senators fan, but it was all because of Mickey Vernon. And not only did that begin my love of baseball, but Mickey became my favorite player."

The influence Vernon had on Kalas' life was not unlike the effect Mickey had on many people's lives. In a quiet way, his good deeds frequently helped or made a difference to countless numbers of people. And the values by which he lived his life were an invaluable model for others.

Certainly one was Mickey's daughter Gay Vernon, a news director at a radio station in Boston. "The values I hold in good stead are not ones I learned from his words per se, but by his example," she said. Among those she mentioned were love, dedication, caring for others, loyalty, generosity, being a good listener, staying in shape, and aging with grace.

"My parents' 63-year marriage was a role model of love and dedication," she added. "A friend once told me that being around them was always magical. There was always fun, music, and dancing in the house, with lots of love and affection."

Mickey practiced his value system well beyond the walls of his own house. At the end of each season, he would pick out a neighborhood kid and give him his baseball glove. He spoke to church groups. He visited the sick. He appeared at schools. And he gave balls and tickets to games to friends and to kids who lived

A devoted family man, Mickey joined wife Lib and 11-month-old Gay for a family activity in 1953.

in the area. Many times, he even stopped at ballfields and gave tips to kids who were playing there.

According to Mickey's sister, Edith Cushman, who's seven years younger, he bought her clothes for each school year and paid the college tuition of some of his relatives. "He was very generous," Cushman said. "Both he and Lib were always doing good. If anyone was sick or needed help, they were always there. They were two of the kindest people we knew."

When Edith gave birth to twin girls right before her birthday, Mickey bought her a clothes dryer. "It was the best gift I ever got," she said. "But that was Mickey. He was always there for me. And we never had an angry word between us, thanks mostly to him, not to me. He was always very supportive."

Television host Maury Povich, whose father Shirley covered the Senators for some 50 years with the Washington *Post*, was a batboy during spring training with the Senators for several years in the late 1940s. Several incidents occurred in Orlando that Povich has never forgotten.

"One time, the boys like me and the players were all out on the field throwing the ball around," he recalled. "We were getting a lot of attention. But my sister, Lynn, was just standing there by herself. Mickey came over, handed her a glove, and played catch with her. He was the only person who did that. He did it intuitively. He didn't want her to be left out.

"I followed Mickey throughout his career," Povich added. "He was my favorite player. I was crushed when he was traded.

"My father used to take me into the clubhouse. One year, he caught me smoking behind the outfield fence at Tinker Field. He said, 'Maybe you should spend more time with Mr. Vernon.'"

When Vernon's good friend, the late Sid Stesis, was in the hospital with a heart attack, Mickey visited him every day. "I don't know of any other person who was more considerate and did more good things for people," said Sid's wife Florence. "He always had time for people, even after he became a celebrity. He never forgot where he came from. He never forgot his family or his friends.

"He was very soft-spoken. He never raised his voice. He never argued," she added. "But when he said something, you know he meant it."

There was a day Vernon was driving through Chester and saw a group of boys playing baseball with old, broken bats and beat-up baseballs. Mickey drove home to Wallingford, rounded up some bats and balls, and returned to the field where he gave the equipment to the surprised youths.

George Case Jr., whose father played with Vernon in Washington and was one of his coaches when Mickey managed there, remembered the time he was beginning a sales career in the sporting goods and athletic footwear business. Case called Vernon to tell him he was going to be in the area, making his first call at a sporting goods store in Media.

"He and Lib invited me to lunch," Case said. "After lunch, Mickey asked me where I was going. When I told him, he asked if he could go with me. Naturally, I said yes. When we got there, Mickey said to the owner, 'This is my friend. I expect you to give him an order.'

"And he did. It was a day I'll never forget.

"Mickey was one of the most popular Washington Senators players of all time," Case added. "Why? Not only because of his talent, but because of his demeanor. He had no pretenses."

"He was the greatest guy I ever knew," said another popular former Senator, ex-third baseman Eddie Yost. "And what a wonderful ballplayer."

When he was a young student at a Ridley Township school, Tim Murtaugh chose to do an interview with Vernon as a class project. "Mickey came to the school," Danny's son said, "and did an interview that lasted two hours. Afterward, I found that the tape hadn't worked. Mickey came back a few days later to do the whole thing over again."

Vernon was once described as "the kind of guy you'd most like to see your kid ask for an autograph." Former pitcher Lou Brissie, who followed Mickey since he played in Greenville, South Carolina, and still has an article about him that as a youth he had cut out from the local newspaper, took that approach a few steps farther.

"My sons loved baseball, but they never played it much," said Brissie, who hurled mostly with the Philadelphia Athletics. "But if I had a son who was a baseball prospect, I would like him to emulate Mickey Vernon. Why? Because he was good at what he did, he did a good job every day—whether it was batting or fielding—and he was a gentleman. He never did anything on the field that I felt in any way reflected on another player or the game in a negative way. He was just as competitive as the next guy. He just didn't show it outwardly. But the people who played against him knew. He had all the traits that I would've liked my sons to have if they'd played at a professional level."

Sports editor and columnist Al Cartwright, writing in the Wilmington *News-Journal*, once made this observation: "James Barton Vernon would be a fine figure of a man, worthy of the neighbors' praises—if not that of Clark Griffith—if he didn't hit anything."

Of course, baseball in those days—just like many other branches of society—was vastly different from the way it is today. "For one thing, people had more respect for each other," said former Boston Red Sox infielder Johnny Pesky. "Sure, we as players all had strong likes and dislikes, but we got along with each other. The overall atmosphere in the game was so good.

"Mickey Vernon fit right into that era. He was a good person. In fact, they were all good people with the Senators. They were seldom in the pennant race, but they busted their butts anyway. No one did that more than Mickey. He didn't make a lot of noise, but he played hard. And he was just a wonderful guy, the kind of guy you couldn't help but like. If all the players today were like Mickey, they would certainly have a lot fewer problems."

Bob Wolff, a Hall of Famer who broadcast Senators games in the 1950s and 1960s, expressed his admiration for Mickey another way. "He was very modest," he said. "He brushed aside compliments. He was not a showoff. We chatted often. He was like having a brother or an uncle."

This, of course, is not to say that Vernon was always perfect. He had a few fights in his day. And he was thrown out of a few games.

"Vernon's quiet demeanor hides a strong competitive spirit, and umpires have felt his wrath from time to time," penned Bill Deekens in *The Sporting News.*

Mickey was thrown out of games four times in his big league career. Twice it happened when he was a player and twice it occurred when he was a coach.

As a player, Vernon was tossed from a game by umpire Ed

Runge after disputing a call at first base. The other ejection came in a much more circuitous fashion.

"George Pipgras, the old Yankees pitcher, was umpiring, and he got into an argument with our manager, Bucky Harris," Vernon said. "He threw Harris out of the game. The following year Pipgras was at first and there was a close play in which he called the batter safe. I disputed the call. I had heard what Bucky said to Pipgras the previous year, so I said to him, 'Do you remember what Bucky told you last year? Well, that goes for me, too.' I got thrown out."

While a coach with the Pittsburgh Pirates, Vernon was invited to take an early shower over a disputed call at first. Another time while serving as a coach with the Montreal Expos, he was tossed after making a remark from the dugout.

In 1946, with the Senators, Vernon had a well-publicized fight with Washington second baseman Gerry Priddy in the locker room. The battle came after Mickey had made a crucial error during a game against the Detroit Tigers.

"Priddy came into the clubhouse and went to the manager to complain about me," Vernon said. "I didn't think he should have done that. He should've come to me. When he came back, he said something to me, and I took a swing at him. He shoved me into a locker. George Myatt stepped between us and tried to break it up. But as he was doing that, I came out of the locker and took another swing at Priddy. I hit Myatt right in the nose."

Vernon's other skirmish in the majors happened when the Cleveland Indians' Bobby Avila hit a grounder to Senators shortstop Pete Runnels and was thrown out by about 10 feet. As he crossed the bag, Avila spiked Mickey, who then grabbed him around the neck and was about to sock him when an umpire intervened.

Mickey also had a brief tussle in the minors while he was playing with Jersey City. Vernon fell while rounding third. He got up and tried to score, but the opposing catcher had charged up the line with the ball. "He blocked me, then knocked me over," Mickey recalled. "I didn't think it was a very good play on his part. I got up and took a swing at him. Dusty Cooke was in the on-deck circle. He grabbed both of us in a bear hug. 'Now, break it up, boys,' he said."

Overall, Vernon's anger was seldom on display. "I never saw him really get mad, never heard him curse," said Matt Zabitka, who for many years wrote about Vernon in the Chester (later the Delaware County) *Times*. "He had a demeanor that everybody loved."

Zabitka added that he once attended opening day in Washington when Vernon was managing the Senators, and shortly before the game, Mickey stopped what he was doing and gave the writer a tour of the clubhouse.

In Delaware County where Vernon is virtually deified, an entire league has been named after him. The Mickey Vernon Little League began in 1955 in Linwood, and has flourished ever since. Today, it is one of the oldest little leagues in the nation and has some 250 players. Each year, Vernon attends the league opener and throws out the first ball. Then he signs autographs and chats with the players and their parents. Sometimes, Mickey also shows up at games unannounced. The league carries his career statistics on its web site.

"The kids just love him," said Joe Montalvo, a former president of the league. "We always make them aware of who he is, and tell them if they work hard enough, they might become a player like he was. To many of the local people, he's like a folk hero."

Mickey commands a high level of admiration with other local people, too. For instance, Billy (White Shoes) Johnson, an outstanding football player who showed his skills at Widener University (previously called PMC) before going on to a glittering career with the Houston Oilers and Atlanta Falcons, grew up across and down the street from Mickey in Marcus Hook.

Johnson's father Leonard was a policeman in Hook for 25 years, and his uncle, Pearlie Johnson, played baseball in the Negro League for about 22 years. From their stories about Mickey, Johnson was well-aware of his existence, even as a youngster.

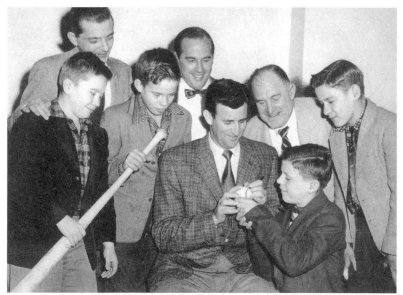

Always willing to make visits in the community, Mickey Vernon spent some time during the off-season in 1955 signing autographs at Elwyn Training School.

"When I finally got a chance to meet him, it was quite a thrill," recalled Johnson, who now works in the Falcons' front office. "Later, I considered it such an honor to know him."

Johnson, once a talented baseball player himself, is much younger than Vernon, and Mickey no longer lived in Marcus Hook when Billy was a youngster. But that didn't stop him from developing an appreciation for the neighborhood star. "He was a role model for me as far as setting goals goes," Johnson said. "I saw how a guy from Marcus Hook could make it. That made it all seem possible."

Whenever Vernon returned to Marcus Hook to visit, "everybody knew when he came to town," Johnson said. "That was the kind of attention he attracted. But he was so down to earth, so congenial. Here was a guy who had all kinds of success as an athlete, yet he was still humble. It's very nice to see somebody from a professional level who's like that."

Vernon's good citizen practices extended well beyond the boundaries of Delaware County. In Washington, for instance, he was often asked to attend little league clinics on Saturday mornings. "I can ask some players and know exactly what they'll say," Senators public relations director Howard Williams told a reporter. "They'll say, 'How much is in it?' But Mickey, all he says is, 'What time?'"

Williams mentioned the time he sent Vernon to participate in an all-night telethon for cerebral palsy. "He didn't have to be coaxed," Williams said. "He never does."

Vernon was accommodating in other ways, too. "My father was an avid duck hunter," said Case, "but Mickey didn't hunt. Yet, every off-season, he'd agree to go duck hunting with my dad at Barnegat Bay. They'd get up at 3:30 a.m., then sit in a cold, wet duck blind for hours on end. I don't think duck hunting had any appeal to Mickey. He just did it to be nice to my dad."

Former Senators pitcher Sid Hudson added another dimension to the character of the man with whom he once roomed and later served as one of his coaches. "We were good friends as players, and we've been good friends ever since," Hudson said. "We always got along. One of the things I admired most about Mickey was that he was as honest as could be. Nobody was more honest than he was."

Another former Senators teammate of Mickey's, outfielder Sam Mele, said that Vernon was "a helluva guy to have on your club. He was a real good competitor, and a gentleman. Everybody was his friend. I never heard him say a bad word about anybody. I don't even remember ever hearing him raise his voice."

According to Chubby Imburgia, who grew up in a house across the street from the Vernons in Marcus Hook and who became a lifelong friend of the first baseman, Mickey never turned down an invitation to attend a local banquet. At the peak of his career, Vernon often attended as many as three banquets a week during the off-season. "He always came," Imburgia said, "and he never left early. Mickey was a guy who could never do enough for you."

"If you didn't like Mickey Vernon," Hall of Fame pitcher Bob Feller said, "you didn't like anybody. He was a fine human being, and he didn't have an enemy in the world."

On the banquet circuit in 1954, Vernon took his good friend Sid Stesis to the 50th anniversary bash of the Philadelphia Sports Writers' Association. Many of the top names in sports were there, including Ty Cobb, Tris Speaker, Jimmie Foxx, Chuck Klein, Lefty Grove, Mickey Cochrane, Home Run Baker, Red Grange, Willie Hoppe, Connie Mack, Jack Kelly Sr., and Joe Louis. Mickey was also among the honorees—as was Al Rosen—for having won the American League batting title the year before.

As told by Sid's son Lou, before the dinner began, Vernon and Stesis were walking among the crowd when they spotted Louis. "There's Joe Louis, let's go talk to him, " Stesis said. Vernon held back, but Stesis approached the king of the heavyweight boxers anyway. "Champ, this is Mickey Vernon. He's the American League batting champion," Stesis said. "I know who he is," Louis replied. "Whenever Washington comes to Detroit, I try to get a seat near first base so I can watch him play."

Once in about 1947, Lou Stesis recalled, his father was in downtown Philadelphia and came upon a big commotion with police and a large crowd of people milling about. As it turned out, the attraction was none other than Babe Ruth. Never too shy about doing such things, the elder Stesis yelled to Ruth that he was a friend of Mickey Vernon. "Let him through," Ruth called. He then proceeded to chat with Sid before giving him an autographed baseball, which still resides in the family.

Arthur Richman has been around baseball for 70 years, serving in various capacities with the St. Louis Browns, New York Mets, and New York Yankees, and toiling for 20 years as a sportswriter with the New York *Mirror* where he became good friends with Vernon. They first met when Vernon was coming up to the big leagues. Over the years, they often had dinner together, or Richman would get tickets for Mickey to Broadway shows.

"He was one of the finest human beings I met in all my years in baseball," said Richman. "There was no one like Mickey Vernon. He shouldn't even have been in baseball. He should've been in the White House."

After he retired, Mickey and Lib attended church every Sunday. In later years, they went with Chuck Taylor, a lifelong friend of the Vernons, who as a youth was a member of a Sunday School class taught by Lib. "I couldn't ask for a better life, being around this guy all these years," said Taylor. "I feel truly blessed."

The Boston Red Sox's fine pitcher Mel Parnell also held Vernon in high esteem. "I feel honored to have had him as a friend and a teammate," he said. "He is a wonderful individual who always commanded great respect in the clubhouse. It was a pleasure for me to have been a teammate of his. I look back at him as being one of the best teammates I ever had."

When Vernon played in Washington, Russ White was a young fan sitting in the stands at Griffith Stadium. "I saw my first game in 1950," he said. "We used to chase after the players to get autographs, and I don't think he ever left the parking lot until he'd signed for everybody. He was just as kind as he could be. He was very similar to Sammy Baugh in that they were both heroes to all the kids."

Some years later, White had grown up to become a sportswriter for the Washington *Daily News,* first covering the Senators in the late 1950s, then becoming the beat writer when Vernon was the expansion team's first manager. "I was a kid from the parking lot, just a raw rookie, when I took over the beat," White said. "But he was extremely gracious. He helped me make the transition.

"He was a model of what you'd want as an employee," White added. "He never got angry. He was a family man. He had strong beliefs. And he got along with black players. Washington in those days was not exactly the place where black players wanted to come. Mickey helped them in every way he could.

"I loved baseball, and I was so privileged to have seen him play when I was a child, and as a young man to have covered him," White said. "If somebody erected a Hall of Good, the first person who should go in is Mickey Vernon."

CHAPTER 2

High-Voltage Swatter

There are hitters. And then there are hitters.

Some swing up, some swing down. Some try to muscle the ball, some try to finesse it. Some try to pull it, some try to hit to all fields. Some swing like they are chopping wood, some swing like they are cracking a whip. Some crouch at the plate, some stand up straight.

It takes all kinds of hitters to make a game. Their levels of success vary. And it doesn't matter what they look like or what technique they use. The only thing that counts is that they hit the baseball someplace where no fielder is standing. Or, as Wee Willie Keeler once said, "Hit 'em where they ain't."

For Mickey Vernon, 2,495 hits say that he hit a lot of balls where they ain't. His two batting championships and his .286 lifetime average say that, too.

With a bat in his hand, Vernon was the consummate hitter. His swing was right out of a textbook. The classic stroke.

When Ted Williams returned from military service during the Korean War, he was anxious to see Mickey. "I want to see him

Two-time American League batting champion, Mickey Vernon was one of the premier hitters of his era.

swing," said the best hitter of all time. "I've got to start all over again, and it might help to see him take a few cuts. For rhythm and balance, he's terrific."

During 15 seasons as a regular, Vernon hit .290 or above nine times. Four times he hit more than .300 with a high of .353 when he won his first batting title in 1946. Vernon also led the American League in doubles three times (1946, 1953, and 1954), was second in total bases three times, second in hits and in triples each twice, second in RBI once, third in doubles once, and fifth in slugging average twice. He drove in 80 or more runs 11 times and scored 70 or more runs 11 times.

Overall, Vernon came to bat during his career 8,731 times. He hit 490 doubles and 120 triples while driving in 1,311 and scoring 1,196. Mickey's career slugging average was .428 with 3,741 total bases. He hit .279 (43-for-154) as a pinch-hitter.

Mickey commanded such respect as a hitter that the renowned Satchel Paige once said: "If I was pitching and it was the ninth inning and we had a two-run lead with the bases loaded and Mickey Vernon was up, I'd walk him and pitch to the next man."

Other pitchers held Vernon in similarly high regard. "He was one of the toughest pitchers in the league," said Cleveland Indians Hall of Famer Bob Lemon. "If you struck him out, it was a pretty good day's work."

"He was as good a hitter as I've ever seen with the bat," said Walt Masterson, who played with Mickey on the Senators for all or parts of 11 years and against him for all or parts of five years. "He had great bat control. Good strong hands. There wasn't really anything he couldn't do with a bat in his hands."

How did Vernon get to be such a good hitter? For one thing, he worked at it. Even during the off-season, Mickey spent time focusing on his hitting. A few times, he chopped down trees in a cemetery in an attempt to work on his swing. Another year, he milked cows.

He had exceptional eyesight, and he studied pitchers. "I watched them all the time," Vernon said. "In my mind, I felt I was just as good as the pitcher. You don't have to be an exceptionally smart hitter, but you do have to know a little bit about the pitchers. You have to study the pitcher and know what he's trying to do to you. And you have to have confidence when you step to the plate. I never lacked that. One of the most important things is to have good wrists and good timing, and be aggressive at the plate.

"I'd rather make a big hit than a big fielding play," Vernon added. "That's what it's all about if you're a batter."

When he was with the Indians, Vernon and Cleveland outfielder Tito Francona talked frequently about hitting. "He would always say, hit what you see. If you don't see it, sit down," Francona recalled.

"Vernon is a combination of power hitting and spray hitter," wrote Shirley Povich of the Washington *Post*. "He hits his home runs only when he swings for them. He's the best exponent of hitting to the opposite field. He swings for the fences in Yankee Stadium, Detroit, and St. Louis. In the other parks, he's discreet enough to go merely for the base hit."

His ability as a hitter always made Vernon a problem for opposing pitchers. Many never really mastered the art of pitching to him.

"I pitched more carefully to Mickey Vernon," said Allie Reynolds, an outstanding hurler for one dozen seasons with the Indians and New York Yankees, "than anyone else. He's not one of those powerful guys who's always looking down a pitcher's throat, but he's always ready. And he's always guarding the dish. You pitch him outside, and he hits to left. You pitch him inside, and he can put it out of the park."

Ned Garver, another superb hurler who spent his best years with the St. Louis Browns and Detroit Tigers—even winning 20 games for the last-place Browns in 1951—had the utmost regard for Vernon but traveled a narrow path when he pitched to him.

"[Stan] Musial was a great hitter," Garver explained. " And [Joe] DiMaggio and Williams were two of the best. But for a couple of years, Mickey Vernon was right there. No matter where you pitched him, he hit it. He was just a great hitter.

"He was a better low ball hitter than a high ball hitter," Garver continued. "[Rogers] Hornsby [the Hall of Fame hitter who managed the Browns briefly in 1952], always said to pitch him low. But that was right into his power. If you used a sinker low, he'd hit it to the opposite field. The best way to pitch him was to keep it in on his fists."

Another one of the many moundsmen who had trouble with Vernon was lefthander Lou Brissie, who came back from a World War II mine explosion that ripped apart one of his legs, requiring 23 operations, to become a solid hurler for the Philadelphia Athletics.

"He was very hard to get the ball by," Brissie said. "Sometimes, you can get a hitter to the point where you can slip one by him. But that was very difficult with Mickey Vernon. He always hit the ball somewhere. I found that you had to pitch him in and out and up and down. I didn't have a lot of success with him. He was a very cool guy and he was just very difficult to pitch to. He was tough for all us pitchers. I know I never found a weakness."

Sid Hudson had the same kind of experience when he joined the Boston Red Sox after playing with Vernon at Washington for nearly nine years. "He was a tough batter to pitch to," the righthanded Hudson said. "All lefthanders gave me trouble. I tried to pitch him in and out, up and down. He was a good low ball hitter. I learned to throw a sinker. He would chase it, and I began to get him out. But he could put the bat on the ball. He always made good contact."

Even relievers, whose job was to retire hitters as quickly as possible without fooling around with too many different pitches, had trouble with Vernon. "I tried to change speeds on him, and I didn't have a good fastball, so I tried to pitch away from him," said Tom Ferrick, whose nine-year career was spent with five teams including two with the Senators. "Mickey was a very intelligent hitter, and he had a good stroke. When he went up to the plate, he knew the pitcher he was batting against. He knew how to handle the guy, what to look for. He just didn't go up indiscriminately and swing."

Despite the problems so many pitchers had when they faced Vernon, Mickey had his nemeses, too. Among them he named Bob Feller, Red Ruffing, Spud Chandler, Atley Donald, and Reynolds—all righthanders—and southpaws Hal Newhouser, Whitey Ford, Bill Henry, and the Lefties Grove and Gomez.

"Feller was the best I ever faced, both before and after the war," Vernon said. "Not only his fastball, but his curve were the best in baseball. My first year, I think I faced him 15 times and struck out nine of them. And he had great stamina. You'd think you could get to him by the seventh inning, but he'd still be throwing just as hard in the eighth and ninth.

"Newhouser had a better assortment of pitches, and was very tough, too, although I once went 5-for-5 against him. Actually, they were all tough, as you can tell by some of those years I had. Thornton Lee [another lefty who pitched most of his years with the Chicago White Sox] gave me as much trouble as anybody," Vernon recalled. "His ball moved in on you. I broke at least one bat every time I faced him."

Unlike today, but typical of his era, Vernon was never platooned, never benched because the pitcher threw from the same side from which he batted. "I was never taken out when a left-handed pitcher was on the mound," Vernon said. "Batting against them wasn't the same as batting against righthanders. I always choked up on the bat a little more against lefthanders to make sure I met the ball. But I did better than average against them."

Mickey began his career with a 35-inch, 35-ounce bat. He finished with a 33-33 bat. Bobby Shantz, however, said he always thought that Vernon's bat was longer.

"That thing looked about 40 inches long," said the little left-hander who enjoyed his best years with the Athletics and Yankees. "He and Gene Woodling. Mickey would put that bat out over the edge of the plate and reach anything that was on the outside. I pitched him very carefully, but I couldn't get him out."

Another southpaw who exercised extreme caution when he pitched to Vernon was Mel Parnell, an excellent hurler for the Red Sox in the 1940s and 1950s. "He was a very good contact hitter," said Parnell, a 25-game winner in 1949. "He wasn't a power hitter, but he'd take a good, natural cut and let the long ball take care of itself. He was a smart hitter, very hard to fool, and he could hit the breaking ball very well. I just tried to keep the ball away from him on the outside of the plate."

Vernon hit 172 home runs during his career, including six seasons when he was in double figures. According to the Tattersall/McConnell log of major league home runs, the most homers Mickey hit against any single pitcher was five. He touched both Reynolds and Steve Gromek five times. He hit four each against Vic Raschi, Virgil Trucks, and Early Wynn, and three apiece off the offerings of Ford, Fred Hutchinson, Eddie Lopat, and Bob Turley. Vernon never hit three home runs in one game, but he hit two in a single game three times—in 1949 against

Washington's Mickey Harris, in 1950 against Ford of the Yankees, and in 1951 against New York's Raschi. Vernon blasted two grand slams—one in 1955 off Boston's Tom Hurd and one in 1958 off Detroit's Jim Bunning. He hit 21 homers with two men on base.

One time, Trucks more than got the best of Mickey. The fire-balling righthander, who toiled most successfully with the Tigers and White Sox, once firing two no-hitters in the same season (1952), struck him out four times in one game on 12 pitches. Vernon missed all but one throw, fouling that one off.

Vernon, of course, had his share of slumps. Some lasted entire seasons, such as the ones in 1948 and 1952 when he hit .242 and .251, respectively. Fans and writers criticized Mickey for his off years, but he always bounced back. "During those times," Vernon said, "it was mostly a case of the hits just not falling. Somebody would always be there to catch the ball. I don't think the pitchers were working me any differently."

According to Vernon, it was always tough on him, as well as his teammates, when his team would go on a road trip. "You'd go into Cleveland where you'd have to face Feller, Lemon, Wynn, and [Mike] Garcia," he said. "Then you'd move on to Detroit where you'd face Newhouser, Trucks, Hutchinson, and [Dizzy] Trout. You'd be lucky to come out of it with even a few hits."

Wynn and Vernon always had particularly lively duels. Originally teammates—both of whom first appeared with the Senators in 1939—the two were traded together to the Indians in 1948 and were roommates. But when Mickey returned to Washington in 1950, he and Wynn struck up a friendly rivalry.

The first time the two faced each other after the trade, the Senators were on their way home from St. Louis and stopped off for a series with the Indians. Vernon laced four hits off Wynn, the last one roaring up the middle, knocking the pitcher's glove off.

"Two things Early really hated," Vernon recalled, "were balls hit up the middle and somebody bunting on him. If you did either of those, he'd knock you down the next time you came up. He wouldn't hit you, but he'd make sure you went down.

"After I hit that ball up the middle, Wynn looked over to first base and yelled, 'Roommate, my ass. Next time I see you, you're going down.'"

A while later, Cleveland visited Washington and in one game Wynn was on the mound. The first time Vernon came to bat, down he went as a pitch flew just over his head. "I told you what I was going to do," Wynn hollered at Vernon. "I just wanted you to know I didn't forget."

In 1942, Vernon was described in *Who's Who in the Major Leagues* as "a high-voltage swatter who has terrific potential with the willow. " A few years later, the same publication claimed that Mickey "is an always dependable swatter." Washington *Post* columnist Bob Addie once wrote that Vernon "was feared by every manager and pitcher in the league." Indicative of his skill with the bat, when Vernon came to the Red Sox, he batted cleanup behind Williams.

Another quality that Vernon brought to the diamond—one that is often overlooked—was his speed on the bases. In an era when stolen bases did not weigh heavily in strategic importance, Mickey was, nevertheless, usually among the league leaders in that category. He swiped 25 bases in 1942, ranking second in the league. The following year, his 24 pilfers placed fifth. He also ranked third in the circuit in steals in both 1947 and 1948 and fourth in 1946.

Vernon hit four inside-the-park home runs during his career, including two less than two months apart in 1946. Overall, he scored 1,196 runs. His high was 101 in 1953. Over a 14-year period at the heart of his career, Vernon averaged 77 runs per season, not a bad figure for a guy who played for mostly lower-level teams.

"People often forget, he was a very good base-runner, one of the best in the league," said Eddie Yost, Washington third baseman and Mickey's teammate for 13 years. "He had very good speed, too, and he was a good bunter. "

When he was manager of the Chicago White Sox, Paul Richards said: "Mickey Vernon is one of the smartest base-runners in the game." Richards was referring especially to the way Vernon took leads and to his judgment on the bases.

Once, however, Richards' assessment was a bit off the mark. "It was opening day one year, and we were two runs behind, but had the bases loaded with two outs in the bottom of the ninth," Vernon recalled. "Yogi Berra picked me off first to end the game. If I could've found a hole, I would've jumped right into it."

Vernon was also regarded as a superb bunter, who could push the ball with considerable proficiency down either line. He was especially adept at drag-bunting.

Was Mickey superstitious, as many ballplayers are? "I had some superstitions," he admitted. "If I was hitting well, I always parked my car in the same spot in the players' lot and walked the same path to the clubhouse. I always looked on the ground for pennies. If I found one, I'd put it in my pocket. I always seemed to get a hit when I did that. I used to call those pennies 'base hits.'"

Another facet of Vernon's career that not only gave it longevity but enhanced his performance on the field was his immunity to injuries. In 20 seasons in the big leagues, Mickey never had a serious injury. He suffered a few pulled muscles and charley horses. He also had two sprained ankles, one coming when he was rounding third and slipped on wet grass, the other arriving after he tried to scramble back to second on a pickoff throw by Cleveland catcher Jim Hegan. Vernon's most serious injury occurred when he was hit in the chest by a pitch thrown by lefthander Tommy Byrne. That gave him a cracked rib.

Vernon had surgery only three times during his career—for an appendectomy, to remove a tumor from his mouth, and to repair a fissure. One reporter wrote that that surgery was for a "fish hook."

"One year in Washington we had a lot of injuries," Vernon said. "Bucky Harris was talking to a writer. He said, 'Mickey Vernon is disgustingly healthy.'"

The fact that he played much of his career in Washington's Griffith Stadium had a considerable bearing on the kind of hitter

Vernon was. With its 31-foot-high wall in right field and its 407-foot distance down the line in left, the ballpark was not conducive to lefthanded power hitters. Consequently, Vernon did not often swing for the fences. He was more content to pepper singles and doubles around the park.

"That wall is what made me a doubles hitter," he said. "No way I was going to clear that thing on a regular basis. I learned to hit line drives and even to hit ground balls into left field."

Boston Red Sox center fielder Dom DiMaggio said that he always felt that the Washington ballpark benefited Vernon. "When it came to power-hitting, it was a tough park to play in," he said. "But there was lots of room to hit around the field, and for a line drive hitter like Mickey, it helped him."

As could be expected, Griffith Stadium was absent from Vernon's list of favorite parks. At the top of that list was Detroit's Briggs Stadium. "Everybody loved to hit there," he said. "You could see the ball well. When you hit the ball, it always sounded like a rifle shot."

Mickey also had Fenway Park in Boston, New York's Yankee Stadium, Sportsman's Park in St. Louis, and Chicago's Comiskey Park high on his list. "Fenway was not only a good park to hit in," Vernon said, "but it was a good place to play after playing in all that heat in Washington. You could get cool and get rejuvenated. I always liked to go there.

"I hit a couple of home runs in the upper deck in Yankee Stadium. If I'd played in any of those parks, I would've tried to become a different kind of hitter. I would've become more of a home run hitter."

Until the end of Vernon's career, the visiting player who hit the most home runs at Yankee Stadium was Goose Goslin with 32. Vernon was second with 31, followed by Williams with 30.

Bob Wolff, Washington's play-by-play announcer in the 1950s and 1960s, sympathized with Vernon's being stuck for so much of his career with the Senators. "Mickey's problem," he said, "is that he played in Griffith Stadium with that high wall. If he'd played

During a 20-year career, Vernon compiled 2,495 hits and a
.286 batting average.

in Yankee Stadium, he would've been one of the top long-ball hitters. He was in the wrong park."

Wrong park or not, Vernon was a master with the bat in his
hands. And the numbers he posted during his 20 years as a player justify that claim.

CHAPTER 3

The Essence of Grace

There is no image of Mickey Vernon that has lingered longer than that of the lithe first baseman with a baseball glove on his hand. It is an image that to a considerable degree defined his baseball career.

The glove set Vernon apart from most first basemen. The way he used it elevated him to the top rung at his position. Put another way, Vernon's defense was about as good as it gets.

It wasn't, of course, just Mickey's mitt that made him such a good fielder. He knew how to play the position. And he was the classic first baseman. Smooth. Graceful. Stylish. Agile. Elegant. Vernon played first base the way Perry Como sang. He fielded with a velvet touch while gliding around the bag as though he was performing a form of outdoor ballet.

"Mickey is the only man I know in baseball who could play first base in a tuxedo, appear perfectly comfortable, and never wrinkle his suit," said Jack Dunn, an assistant general manager of the Baltimore Orioles in the 1950s.

No first baseman of his era was a better fielder than
Mickey Vernon.

"He played so flawlessly that he made it look easy," Morris
Siegel once wrote in the Washington *Daily News*. "He was the
essence of grace."

Vernon, who had the added qualities of speed, good reflexes,
considerable range, and the gift of being able to make backhand-
ed stops with ease, was such a sight to behold with the glove that
people even came early to the ballpark to watch him take infield
practice. Consider the implications. In a sport dominated by hitters, how many players ever attracted such attention with their
defensive skills?

When he played, Vernon had few peers at first base. Perhaps
Eddie Waitkus and George McQuinn were close. But no one else
was remotely comparable. And among more recent first basemen,
certainly Vernon gets only a little competition from the band of

mostly cloven-hoofed pretenders who are sent to stumble around the initial sack because the position is regarded as the one of least liability.

The way Vernon handled the leather and cavorted around the bag, for much of his career with the familiar "W" on his Washington Senators uniform flapping on his chest, was a talent that seemed to come naturally. Only someone born with such ability could perform so adroitly. Or was there something else?

"I worked at it," said Vernon, whose only equal as a first baseman in Washington annals was one of his predecessors, Joe Kuhel. "I practiced all the time. I took grounders, made throws. Most of my errors were on throws. I didn't pattern myself after anybody. Fielding sort of came naturally. It was just me. But I didn't get where I did without a lot of hard work."

Vernon worked especially hard during spring training. He worked on his fielding, but most of all he worked on his throws. After the day's regular work was done, he'd grab another infielder and take him to the diamond where he'd practice his throws. Mickey practiced throwing to third after fielding a bunt. He practiced throwing to second after fielding a bunt.

"Sometimes, I'd also get somebody to throw balls in the dirt so I could practice scooping the ball up," he said. "During the season, I always had the groundskeeper take more sod out around the bag and replace it with dirt. It was easier to scoop a ball out of dirt than it was out of grass."

Mickey preferred the throws to come at him chest high. But he could scoop up a ball with astonishing ease. And he could move skillfully to either side of the bag to snare wide throws. Those were talents that were not lost on his fellow infielders, who could make throws to first with the confidence that even if they chucked a bad one, Vernon would most likely track it down.

Eddie Yost was one of those infielders. Like Mickey, Yost was one of Washington's top players while performing from 1947 through 1958 as the Senators' third baseman. Yost, who overall enjoyed an 18-year career in the big leagues, could field a ball and fire it to first without concern about whether or not it would be caught.

"I wasn't really too accurate with my throws," he recalled. "My ball had a tendency to go in a little and down a little. Often, Mickey had to dig my throws out of the dirt. But I could throw over to first base and not have to worry about it. I knew he would catch it."

Third baseman Al Rosen, who teamed with Vernon when they played together with the 1949-50 Cleveland Indians, was similarly confident when he shot a throw to first.

"When you're playing third base, you always like to have somebody at first who can dig it out," he said. "Mickey certainly could do that. I remember in 1950, he saved me two throwing errors. He could really play."

Infielder Johnny Pesky played with Vernon only briefly in Washington in 1954, but he saw him in action as an opponent for many years before that. "All you had to do was throw the ball near him, and he'd get it," said the one-time shortstop of the Boston Red Sox. "He was a terrific first baseman, one of the best of all time. He had good hands, he had good feet, meaning he could easily shift in any direction. He could do everything around the bag."

Over the years, Vernon prevented countless numbers of infielders from being charged with countless numbers of errors. At the same time, he also kept his own errors to a minimum.

During his entire career, Vernon committed just 212 errors. And they were spread over 2,237 games at first base. He had a lifetime fielding percentage of .990.

Although his error total was unusually low for a first baseman, Vernon did lead the American League in miscues once (1942) and tied for the league lead twice (1946 and 1947). But he also led first basemen in fielding percentage three times—in 1951, 1952, and 1954—and tied for the lead in 1950. His highest marks were in 1951 and 1955 when he fielded .994.

Unlike many muscle-bound first basemen of today, Vernon's glove made him indispensable. Mickey played first base in 150 or more games in eight different seasons, four times appearing in every one of his team's games—twice when they numbered 154, once at 152 and once at 151. From 1942 to 1949 with two years out for the service, Vernon missed only 18 of his team's games, and from 1951 to 1955 he failed to appear in just 19 games in which his club played.

Vernon ranked first in the AL three times in putouts (1949, 1953, and 1954), three times in double plays (1941, 1953, and 1954), and once in assists (1949). In 1949, he set career highs in putouts with 1,438 and in assists with 155.

Among first basemen, Vernon holds the major league career record for participating in the most double plays. He took part in 2,044 twin-killings. He also holds American League career records for most games played (2,227), most chances (21,198), most putouts (19,754), most assists (1,444), and most double plays (2,041).

With such records, it is easy to describe Vernon as a pitcher's best friend. Walt Masterson won't quibble with that.

A Philadelphia native, Masterson pitched with the Senators for all or parts of 11 seasons, eight of which he was Vernon's roommate. "He's the best first baseman I ever saw," said the veteran of 14 big league seasons. "I never saw anybody that good with the glove."

Masterson said that one of Vernon's many assets was his ability to come across the bag for a throw. "He was the best there was at getting the throw with the runner coming down the line," the pitcher said. "He knew exactly where he was. If the throw was on the foul side, he would move right across the bag and get it. And nobody ever ran into him."

At least, most of the time. "Well, sometimes I'd get bumped a little," Vernon said. "But I always thought I had to catch the ball, no matter where it was."

Once, Vernon had to go high for a throw. "Bob Kennedy ran into me like a football player," Mickey said. "I had a sore chest for a month. Another time, when I was with Washington, the Indians' Al Smith hit a ball, and I had to leap up in the air for the throw and make a swipe tag. It was a tough call, but the umpire called Smith out. Cleveland's manager Al Lopez came running out of the dugout to argue. I said, 'Al, I got him on the elbow.' Al said, 'That's good enough for me,' and he turned and ran back to the dugout."

When Boston's Mel Parnell pitched his no-hitter against the Chicago White Sox in 1956, Vernon was involved in a critical play even though he never touched the ball. With two outs and a man on first, pinch-hitter Walt Dropo hit a hard bouncer back to the mound. Parnell fielded his former teammate's shot, but instead of throwing to Vernon at first for the final out, ran the ball over to the bag and made the putout himself. It was the first time a no-hitter ever ended with the pitcher recording the final out.

"After I crossed the bag, Mickey turned and looked at me kind of funny," Parnell recalled. "He said, 'What's the matter, you don't trust me with the ball?' I said, 'Mickey, I have all the confidence in the world in you. I just didn't want to risk throwing it over your head.'

"Mickey was a great fielder, though," Parnell continued. "He could make all the plays. Having a guy like that behind you was a big asset to a pitcher because it helped him decide how he wanted to pitch to the batter. If it was a lefthanded batter, for instance, you wanted to pitch him inside and try to get him to hit the ball to Mickey."

Vernon seldom gave umpires any trouble. In fact, American League umps used to say that Mickey griped the least about calls of all first basemen in the circuit.

It wasn't that Mickey never spoke. He always enjoyed conversations with batters when they reached first base. That practice, however, was eventually stopped.

"I usually said something to guys when they reached base," Vernon recalled. "One day, I came into the clubhouse and there was a memo attached to my locker. It was from Clark Griffith. It said, 'You are talking entirely too much to the other players at first base. It doesn't look good in the stands. If it continues, I am going to take some of your money.'

"I had a reason for talking," Vernon continued. "Sometimes you'd say something to a guy and he might miss a sign or step off the base. But after Griffith's memo, I didn't do it any more. They had a no-fraternization rule then anyway. During batting practice a couple of umpires would come out to see if any players were conversing with opposing players. If they caught you talking, you'd be fined. Once, I was fined $15."

Whether he was talking or not talking, Vernon always paid particular attention to the base-runner anyway. And he had a special way of covering first base on attempted pickoff throws. "Mickey always wanted to tag the runner in the chest," Masterson remembered. "Normally, when a runner back then was trying to get back to first on a pickoff play, he stuck his feet out first. Mickey figured if you tug him in the chest, you'd have a good chance of getting him out. He always told the umpire, 'We're going to tag him in the chest, so don't watch his feet.'

"We worked on that play a lot," Masterson added. "It had other advantages, too. One was that a runner wouldn't get too far off base. That made it good for getting double plays. "

One play over which Vernon had no control and which turned into tragedy occurred during a game in the early 1940s. According to Bill Gilbert in his book, *They Also Served*, third baseman Sherry Robertson, a nephew and adopted son of Clark Griffith and a newcomer in the lineup, made a wild throw to first that was so high it flew over the glove of a leaping Vernon and sailed into the stands. The throw hit a man in the head. After treatment, he walked out of Griffith Stadium on his own, then went to the emergency room of a nearby hospital. That night, the man died.

Vernon was not reluctant to give advice to other players about how to play his position. He often gave tips to young players, even ones from opposing teams. When Vernon was sidelined with an ankle injury while playing with Washington, manager Bucky Harris called on outfielder Sam Mele to man the initial sack. "I'd never played first in my life," said Mele, who claimed that Vernon was not only a great fielder but one who was especially skilled at making the double play and who he never remembered making a bad throw. "But I told Harris I could do it. And Mickey gave me some good suggestions."

In that same period, Vernon participated in several other unusual events. These had happy endings. On August 16, 1943, he participated in a record 10 double plays in a 23-inning double-header. Then on May 29, 1946, he made two unassisted double plays in one game.

According to the major league triple play database assembled from the research of Herm Krabbenhoft, Jim Smith, and Steve Boren, Vernon also took part in two triple plays as a fielder. On September 14, 1941, in the second inning against the Detroit Tigers, he crept in for a bunt with Pinky Higgins at bat. But instead of bunting, Higgins smoked a drive down the line. Vernon leaped and caught it—thus robbing Higgins of at least a double—turned and touched first to retire Bruce Campbell, then threw to shortstop Cecil Travis covering second to get Rudy York trying to scramble back to the bag. From then on, Higgins always kidded Vernon about the play. "How could you play me for a bunt?" he would say. "I never bunted."

Mickey's other triple play occurred on May 22, 1952, with the New York Yankees at bat in the ninth inning. Irv Noren lined to Senators' pitcher Bob Porterfield, who wheeled and threw to Vernon at first to get pinch-runner Art Schult. Vernon then fired to shortstop Pete Runnels covering second to nail Andy Carey diving back to the bag. The play ended the game.

Like all of his other sparkling exploits at first base, these were glowing testaments to the skill and grace with which Vernon played his position. They did not go unnoticed.

"He was the most graceful player I ever saw," said television host Maury Povich, who grew up in Washington while his father Shirley covered the Senators. "I've never seen grace like that on a baseball field. There was only one other player who compared with Mickey Vernon in that area, and that was Joe DiMaggio."

Vernon was the essence of elegance around the bag.

CHAPTER 4

The Kid from Marcus Hook

The tiny borough of Marcus Hook, just 1.14 square miles in size, sits hard by the Delaware River near the southeastern tip of Pennsylvania. Only a few miles above the Delaware border, and about 20 miles south of Philadelphia, it is one of many municipalities that are part of Delaware County, the smallest but third most populated county in the state.

The earliest known settlers took up residence in Marcus Hook in the 1640s. Originally, the town was called Marraties Hoeck, the first word presumed to be the name of a local Indian chief, the last name being a Dutch word meaning "corner" or "point."

In 1701, an "official" town was created under a charter by William Penn. It wasn't until 1892, however, that the borough was incorporated.

During the late 17th and early 18th centuries, Marcus Hook— a corrupted version of the town's original name—was a haven for pirates. They often rendezvoused there. The notorious pirate, Blackbeard, was said to have frequented the area. One of its streets was named Discord Lane because of the many brawls and riots between pirates, as well as the local citizens, that occurred on the thoroughfare.

In its heyday, Marcus Hook was a thriving industrial community with a number of plants lining the river's edge. One of the earliest businesses was shipbuilding. Later, oil refineries emerged along with manufacturing businesses that produced goods such as linoleum, oil cloth, silk, and barrels.

Tankers, barges, and cargo vessels dotted the waterfront. To accommodate the many seamen who constantly came ashore, Marcus Hook at one point boasted 22 saloons. Stores and houses covered most of the remaining inland areas of the town. Most of the adult males in the borough worked at one of the big companies along the river.

Since the late 1800s, the population of Marcus Hook ranged from 1,000 to a high of more than 5,000 in the 1920s. Its present population, whose residents are called "Hookers," is about 2,300.

Sports played a major role in the lives of Hookers. Baseball was especially popular with teams and leagues for all ages and at all levels available to the male population. Some of the teams were even considered "semipro."

It was this environment that developed not only the finest athlete ever to come out of Marcus Hook, but arguably the best and surely the most decorated athlete ever to emerge from the ranks of sports-rich Delaware County.

He was born James Barton Vernon. To everyone, he was simply "Mickey." Mickey Vernon, the kid from Marcus Hook, would go on to become a local baseball legend.

Born April 22, 1918 in his parents' house at Third and Green Streets, Mickey and his family soon moved to a house owned by Sun Oil Company at 507 Green Street.

James' parents were Marcus Hook natives. As did his grandfather, a carpenter who worked on many of the houses in Marcus Hook, Mickey's father Clarence carried from an unknown source the nickname of "Pinker." The younger Pinker was a standout baseball and soccer player as a young man. He worked all his life

A youthful Mickey as a 10-year-old (front, third from right) got together with some members of his family, including his mother Kate (back, third from left) and sister Edith (bottom left).

in what localites call "Hook," first at Viscose Company, a 12-block walk from his house, then starting in 1919 at Sun Oil where he would spend the next 43 years as a stillman and later a jitney driver. Mickey's mother, nee Katherine (Kate) Morris, was one of nine children, eight of them girls. She, too, worked at Sun Oil as a young woman. Both Vernons worked six days a week, 12 hours a day, and were paid $12 a week.

The Vernons had three children. James, named after an uncle, James McAbee, was the middle child. An older brother, Clarence, died of pneumonia at nine months of age. A sister, Edith, was born seven years after Mickey.

Mickey, of course, was not always Mickey. That name was given to him by an aunt when he was three years old.

"There was a song called *Mickey*, and I used to play it over and over on the Victrola," Vernon recalled. "My aunt Helen Konegan started calling me Mickey, and the name stuck. Soon everybody was calling me that."

Young Mickey attended Green Elementary School at Seventh and Green Streets until partway through third grade when his parents moved into one of Jim McAbee's two houses in nearby Boothwyn. Mickey lived there from the age of eight to 14, attending Boothwyn Elementary School through eighth grade.

As Mickey was about to start ninth grade, his family moved back to Marcus Hook because his mother apparently wasn't happy living in Boothwyn away from her many relatives. The house into which the family moved stood at 816 Eighth Street on a block where two other Vernon families also lived. Mickey would spend the rest of his early years in that house.

Because Marcus Hook didn't have a high school of its own, students had a choice of attending either Eddystone or Ridley Park High Schools, both of which were located north of Chester. Mickey chose Eddystone.

By then, baseball had entered Mickey's life. At an early age, the youngster attended games in which Pinker played. Pinker was an outstanding hitter and first baseman for the Sun Oil team, which played in a fast Delaware County league.

"The ballfield was right near the refinery," Mickey said. "My dad would take me to his games, but then during the games, he'd figure it was time for me to go home. I was only little at the time. My dad would give a quarter or a half-dollar to somebody to take me home."

The young Vernon didn't play much baseball himself. "While living in Marcus Hook, I hardly ever played," he said. "I never played on a field. When we did play, it was in the street with neighborhood kids like Bill and Tom Ross."

One thing the youngster did do with some frequency was ride horses. "My Uncle Jim [McAbee] had a little farm on Post Road in Marcus Hook," he said. "He had horses. Once, he gave me a horse. At the time, our house in Marcus Hook had a small, wooden fenced-in yard in the back. Uncle Jim let me take the horse home. I rode it home, and put it in the back yard. When my mother saw it, she made me take it back. The horse died the next day."

When his family moved to Boothwyn, Vernon's interest in baseball began to expand. Largely rural at the time, the area had lots of open spaces. Kids had opportunities to entertain themselves in many different ways. Like all kids used to do, they invented games to play. And they also played baseball.

"I played on my first real field after we moved to Boothwyn," Vernon said. "That area had many fields. In the summer, you'd play either baseball or go swimming. I even played on a grade school team on Bergdoll Field. But I didn't take baseball too seriously."

The first time that Mickey ever wore a baseball uniform was when he was 14 years old and played for a team sponsored by Linwood Methodist Church, which his family attended. According to Vernon, the best player on the team was center fielder Joe Hinson, who later played in the Negro League.

At the age of 15, Vernon entered 10th grade at Eddystone High. The school, however, had no baseball team. So Mickey played on the basketball team. That endeavor lasted only until a doctor discovered that Vernon had a heart murmur and forbade him to play the sport.

But Mickey was allowed to play baseball. That summer, he joined an American Legion league in Marcus Hook and played for a team sponsored by C. L. Morris Furniture Store. John Long was the manager.

"I always played right field," Mickey recalled. "I was too small to play first base. I was the smallest guy on the team and batted leadoff. Our team was disqualified from the playoffs because we had somebody who was too old."

As he was beginning to play more baseball, Mickey was also developing another closely related interest: major league baseball.

Pinker was one of several people who helped to cultivate that interest. "My dad did all the things dads do with kids," Mickey said. "He was always available to have a catch. And he often took me to Shibe Park to see the Athletics and to Baker Bowl to see the Phillies. It was then that I decided I wanted to become a baseball player."

Mickey's uncles (Jim McAbee and Dave Morris) also frequently took him to major league games in Philadelphia. To this day, Vernon considers them and his dad his most important role models.

Harold (Liz) Knox, who lived in a house on Mallon Avenue

behind the Vernons, remembered the long hours Mickey spent playing baseball at the local ballfield. "He was just a tall, lanky kid, and he had a very long reach," said Knox, who's five years Vernon's senior. "In the summer he would spend all day on the field, hitting and shagging balls. If you wanted to see him, you went to the field. He practiced there all the time.

"After a while," Knox added, "he started to draw a crowd. He was a good, natural fielder, and he didn't back away from anything that was hit at him, no matter how hard it was. He could hit, too. We had some real good players in Marcus Hook, and Mickey was one of them. You could tell that he was going to go places as a player. When he took over first base on the Legion team, he looked like he was made for the position."

When Mickey got a little older, he and friends hitchhiked to Shibe Park, a difficult trip, considering they were going from Marcus Hook all the way to the north side of Philadelphia.

"We'd pack lunch and leave early in the morning," Vernon said. "We traveled up Chester Pike into West Philadelphia, then passed the zoo, up Girard Avenue to Broad Street, then north to Lehigh Avenue where we'd either walk or ride the final seven blocks to the ballpark. We did a lot of walking. It would be late at night when we'd finally get back home.

"The player I liked best was Jimmie Foxx," Vernon added. "He hit those long home runs. I liked Mickey Cochrane and Charlie Gehringer, too. I also remember seeing Ty Cobb and Babe Ruth."

Hitchhiking was the way kids often got around in those days, and Mickey and his pals were not averse to making longer trips than the one to Shibe Park. In 1933, when he was 15 years old, Vernon and three friends, including his future best man, George (Shorty) Baldwin, hitchhiked all the way to Washington to see the Senators and the New York Giants in the World Series. They wound up seeing two games.

"Hitchhiking was no problem," Vernon remembered. "Of course, we had no tickets. So we took turns standing in line all night for bleacher tickets. Two of us would stand in line and two of us would go across the street to a café. Then we'd switch places. We finally got seats in right-center field in some temporary bleachers under the flag pole."

Meanwhile, Vernon's own baseball activities were increasing. When he was 16, Pinker took him to Chester to try out for an American Legion team. Mickey made the team. So did a kid who lived at Third and Lloyd Streets in Chester named Danny Murtaugh. And a lifelong friendship was born.

"I had seen him before that when we both played basketball in a church league," Vernon recalled. "He was a good basketball player. He was a guard, and was very tough to score on. He was like a leach. He was just a little guy, but with a lot of hustle.

"When we made the Legion team together, he played second base and I played first and batted cleanup. It was the first time I had ever played first base, but I knew I wanted to play there. There were only three positions a lefthander could play—first base, pitcher, and outfield—and I knew I didn't want to pitch or play the outfield. There was a lot more action at first base."

Vernon learned the position by watching how others played it. Soon, word of Mickey's baseball prowess was starting to spread. And Vernon wanted to step up a few notches. In an article in the Chester *Times*, Arnold (Lefty) Vann, a noted local baseball figure and manager of a fast-paced team from Congoleum-Nairn, a large manufacturing company in Marcus Hook, told this story:

"We had a game scheduled in New York on a Sunday to play a team called the Brooklyn Farmers," recalled Vann, referring to an all-star team from Chester that he also managed. "The day before the game, this very young, tall, skinny kid came over to the plant looking for me. Someone directed him to the plant yard and he ambled over to the warehouse platform where I was standing. 'My name's Mickey Vernon,' he said. 'I'd like to play with Chester in New York tomorrow.'

"I knew all about the kid's great playing ability and his reputation as a classy first baseman," Vann said. "I hated to refuse the kid because he was so eager to play." Vann told Vernon he could

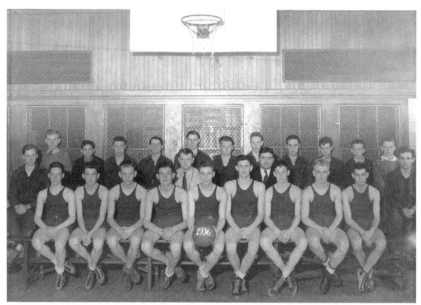

The 1936 Eddystone High School basketball team featured Mickey Vernon (front, fourth from right). Coach Wilmer Frye sits in middle (light shirt).

come, but he would have to play right field because the team had a regular first baseman.

At the game the next day, Vernon was, as Vann promised, stationed in right field. The shortstop on the Brooklyn team was Don Kellett, who later became general manager of the Baltimore Colts. In the late innings, a grounder got through Mickey's legs, and cost Chester the game. Despite the error, Vann gave Vernon $8 for his troubles, marking the first time Mickey was paid for playing baseball.

His "professional" status notwithstanding, Vernon went back to Eddystone, a school that closed its doors in the 1960s. He played no football because Pinker said, "If you get hurt playing football, you might not ever play baseball." But as a senior he was allowed to resume playing basketball, and he performed with distinction on the high school team.

During the regular season, Eddystone, under coach Wilmer Frye, posted a 7-8 record, averaging 19.1 points per game, while playing high schools such as Chester, Radnor, and now-defunct

In 1935, young Vernon (front, second from right) played with a fast-paced team from Sun Oil.

ones including Media, Swarthmore, Collingdale, Ridley Park. Glen-Nor, Prospect Park, St. Robert's, and Clifton Heights. Considered tall at 6 feet, 2 inches, Mickey was the team's center. In an annual Christmas tournament sponsored by the Chester Kiwanis Club and including many of the local high schools, Eddystone won three preliminary games to reach the final before losing a 23-19 decision to Springfield. Vernon scored nine points, and was named to the all-tournament team.

There was still no baseball at Eddystone, so Vernon at ages 17 and 18 spent the summers playing with the semipro Sun Oil team in the Delaware River Industrial League. In one game, Mickey faced former Phillies pitcher Lefty Weinert, who was playing for Rees Malloy, and laced two hits off him. Another time, Vernon played against a team led by former Boston Red Sox infielder Bill Narleski, whose son Ray later became a teammate of Mickey's on the Cleveland Indians.

While he played for Sun Oil, Vernon also had a summer job with the company. One year, he had a job that required him to walk the pipeline, looking for leaks. It was a trip that stretched three and one-half miles from the refinery in Marcus Hook, through woods, and to a tank farm in Twin Oaks. "I never saw anything that even resembled a pinhole," Mickey remembered.

As a teenager, Vernon seldom made any noise except on the baseball field. "He was very quiet," his sister Edith Cushman said. "You never heard him sass anybody. He had many of my father's characteristics. Like my father, he was not very aggressive, but he was always anxious to help people. After my father retired, he would baby-sit the kids of seamen whose wives were working. He was always baby-sitting for relatives when they were in a jam. He was a very kind man, and Mickey was just like him."

When he was a student at Eddystone, Vernon was asked by a teacher what he wanted to do with his life. Mickey responded that he wanted to be a professional baseball player.

That dream flirted with the possibility of becoming a reality when Mickey had a tryout with the Phillies at Baker Bowl during his senior year at Eddystone.

"I worked out every day for one week with eight or 10 other kids," Vernon said. "I never swung a bat. Just fielded. It went all right, but they didn't offer me a contract. I only weighed 150 pounds, so I guess they didn't think much of such a frail fellow."

Vernon, who never had a tryout with the Athletics, graduated from Eddystone in June 1936. The school yearbook noted that he had played basketball, baseball (which was really for a pickup team that had played a few games against other schools), spent three years in the glee club, performed in the operetta, and was vice president of the freshman class. "Tall, dark and handsome he, baseball's his specialty," read the notation next to his picture.

Just how much of a specialty baseball had become in Vernon's life was even more apparent when he was offered a scholarship to Villanova University. It would be the first major step in Mickey's climb to the top.

CHAPTER 5

On the Way Up

Mickey Vernon did not intend to go to college. It just turned out that way.

College in the 1930s, after all, wasn't for baseball players with professional aspirations. Maybe a few players attended institutions of higher education. But for the most part, if a kid wanted to pursue a career in baseball, the typical path was to get out of high school, join a team at a lower level of the minor leagues, and hope you were good enough to climb the ladder to the big leagues.

Besides, Vernon had been a vocational student at Eddystone High School. And by his own admission, he "was not a very good student." College was not in his plans.

But that was before he met George (Doc) Jacobs.

Jacobs was the head baseball coach at Villanova University. He had heard about this classy kid from Marcus Hook who played baseball with the grace of a ballet dancer and the style of a concert pianist. Although he was just 17 years old, the boy was already performing far above his age level, playing with grown men in a fast semipro league in lower Delaware County. It was the second year that the youngster had played in the league, and by all accounts he had a big future in baseball.

Jacobs had to have a look. So on a warm summer night in 1936, he drove from the Main Line campus down to Marcus Hook to watch the kid play first base for Sun Oil. The coach wasn't disappointed. Soon afterward, he offered Vernon a scholarship to Villanova.

The Wildcats in those days were no pushovers in baseball. Future big leaguers such as Lenny Merullo, Frank Skaff, Ben Geraghty, Nick Etten, Ray Stoviak, Mike Garbark, and Art Mahan, as well as Art Raimo, later a prominent football coach, all played baseball at Villanova in the 1930s. According to Mahan, a future Villanova baseball coach and athletic director, the college nine was not only as prominent as the basketball team but was one of the top squads in the country and even gave out financial aide to some of its players. Villanova was a good place to play baseball, and in the fall of 1936 Vernon was welcomed with open arms.

Mickey breezed through the admissions process, was placed in the school of engineering, and given football star Buzz Howlett as a roommate. Then the semester began.

"I was in class one day and the professor asked me to go to the blackboard and do a problem," Vernon recalled. "I fumbled around, and he said, 'You don't know how to do this, do you?' He said I was wasting his time. So I figured I'd better try something else. I went over to commerce and finance, which was Howlett's major, but after two days of going to classes, they caught me and took me out of that department."

When Jacobs learned about Vernon's academic dilemma, he told Mickey he'd see what he could do. And what he did was to get Vernon placed in the pre-med program.

Vernon attended classes for the rest of the semester. "Then in the spring," he said, "I just went to practice and played baseball." Because first-year students weren't allowed to play varsity sports in those days, Mickey suited up with the freshman team.

The freshman baseball coach was Bunny Galazin, the center

on the football team. He presided over a team that played not only other college freshman squads, but also high school varsity nines.

One of the teams that Villanova played that year was from North Catholic High School in Philadelphia. The teams met twice, and in one game Vernon went 3-for-4 with a home run in a 2-1 Villanova victory. In the other meeting between the teams, Mickey's homer gave the Wildcats a 1-0 decision.

In both cases the losing North pitcher was a big righthander from the Juniata Park section of Philadelphia. His name was Walt Masterson, and he was one of the hottest hurlers in the city.

Little did either player realize at the time how closely linked they would become. Several years later, Vernon and Masterson would be roommates with the Washington Senators.

"I didn't know him," said Masterson. "But in 1939, when we both came to Washington, Mickey told me that he was the guy who'd hit those home runs off me at Villanova. After he told me who he was, we developed a special kinship because we came from the same area. We wound up being roommates for eight years. And to this day, we're still very good friends."

Although he spent most of his time with the varsity, Jacobs kept an eye on his young slugger. Villanova notwithstanding, Jacobs had an ulterior motive. He had just taken a summer job as manager of the Easton (Maryland) Brownies, a minor league club in the Class D Eastern Shore League. And he was looking for players.

Easton was the same team that had spawned Jimmie Foxx more than a decade earlier. The club had recently been purchased by Ernest Landgraf, and with the help of Jacobs, who kept his job at Villanova, he had secured a working agreement with the St. Louis Browns.

When the Browns came to Philadelphia that spring for a series with the Philadelphia Athletics, Jacobs arranged a tryout for Vernon at Shibe Park. The pair drove to the park, and as St. Louis first baseman Jim Bottomley watched, Mickey showed what he could do.

"On the way back to Villanova," Vernon remembered, "Jacobs told me I ought to go down to Easton. He said it was a good opportunity. I agreed, and I signed for $80 a month, plus a $400 bonus at the end of the season if I did well."

And so in the spring of 1937, Mickey Vernon began a professional baseball career that would touch on four decades. He was a 6-foot, 2-inch, 155-pound, 19-year-old who had never lived away from home.

"I got a couple of bucks a day for food," Mickey said. "I lived with four or five other guys in a boarding house. The lady who owned the house fed us. We each paid her $4 a week."

Ironically, the tough little Irish kid from Chester who had become one of Mickey's best friends also joined the league that year. Danny Murtaugh, who signed his first contract with the St. Louis Cardinals, was assigned to the Cambridge (Maryland) team.

Although it had been in existence for many years, it's doubtful that the league ever had a more tumultuous season than 1937. Salisbury, also in Maryland, was the top club in the loop, but it was learned that the team had used too many "classmen," the name given to players from a higher level. Teams then were permitted to use just a few players who had been sent down. Because it exceeded that number, Salisbury was forced to forfeit 21 wins, and on June 19 it went from first place to last, its record dropping from 21-6 to 0–27.

Salisbury, however, was down but not out. The club won 48 of its final 58 games to regain first place. It clinched the pennant with a doubleheader win over Easton, which finished in second place with a 56-41 record, three and one-half games out of first. Cambridge wound up in third place. Subsequently, Salisbury won the league playoffs.

For Vernon, it was a year of many adjustments. Playing every day was different. The pitching was different. Nearly everything about playing professionally for the first time was different. Still, Mickey managed to hit .287 in 83 games with 10 home runs and 64 RBI. Oddly, he also led the league in errors with 16. Both he and

Murtaugh, who hit .297, received honorable mention on the all-league team.

Late in the season, St. Louis general manager Bill DeWitt had come to Easton to watch the Brownies play. Ultimately, he declared, "There are no prospects on this team." The Browns decided not to pick up the option they had on Vernon or on any of the other players.

It so happened, however, that the Salisbury team was owned by Joe Cambria, a former operator of a laundry in Baltimore and at the time the owner of several minor league teams as well as a Negro League club, and also an important scout for the Washington Senators. Cambria specialized in signing Latin American players for the team, but he liked what he saw of Vernon, and talked the Senators into buying his contract for $500.

The following February, Cambria appeared at the Senators' minor league training camp in St. Augustine, Florida bearing a turtle that he had caught after seeing it crossing a highway, as well as a report on his new recruit. Washington traveling secretary Billy Smith was not amused. "For weeks you are on the road," he scolded Cambria, "and all you have to show for it is a turtle and another Cuban." Smith was not a fan of Cuban ballplayers who he couldn't understand and who couldn't understand him.

"The boy is not a Cuban," insisted Cambria, who also signed Senators stars George Case and Eddie Yost. "I think he's an Irishman. And he's a college boy from Villanova. You'll be hearing a lot about him one of these days."

"At camp that spring there were 12 or 14 Cuban players," Vernon recalled. "One of them, Gil Torres, called a strike for more meal money. Just the Cubans went on strike. It lasted for a couple of days. We all got another 50 cents."

Mickey had a good spring. And he thought he'd be assigned to Trenton, a Class A team in the Eastern League that was also owned by Cambria. But on the way north, Trenton stopped in Greenville, South Carolina to play an exhibition game against the

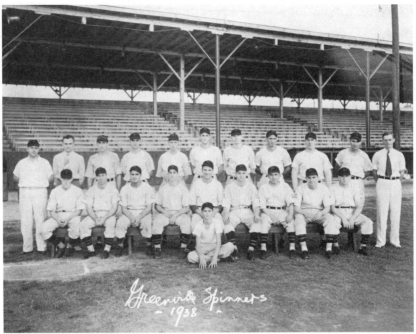

In his second year in the minors in 1938, Mickey (back, sixth from left) was a member of the Greenville (SC) Spinners of the South Atlantic League.

local Spinners in the Class B South Atlantic League. When Trenton left town, Vernon stayed behind.

Before the regular season started, Vernon had the chance to play against the New York Yankees, who also stopped at Greenville for an exhibition game. "Lou Gehrig was still playing," Vernon said. "He was always one of my favorites. But you could tell he was having problems. On one play, Joe Gordon made a low throw from second that Gehrig had trouble with. He yelled over to Gordon to 'get it up.'"

The 1938 Greenville team under manager Jigs Donohue had some talent. Al Brancato, Joe Kohlman, and Les McCrabb were on the team. All appeared later in the big leagues. Another Spinner was the former Villanova infielder, Frank Skaff, who later became a long-time major league coach and managed the Detroit Tigers for part of the 1966 season. "He was a bit older than the rest of us," Vernon recalled. "He kind of took me under his wing."

At one point, Skaff discovered that neither of Mickey's parents had signed his contract, and as a minor, Vernon was therefore actually not supposed to be playing. The league declared Vernon a free agent, and other teams—most notably the Brooklyn Dodgers—attempted to sign him. Mickey declined the offers, and eventually his dad, Pinker, inked his name to the pact. Mickey even got a $25 a month raise out of the deal.

But Greenville couldn't win. And it finished the season buried in last place with a 53-83 record, 25½ games behind the first-place Savannah Indians.

Playing in 132 games, Vernon batted .328, but hit only one home run while driving in 72 and scoring 84. In one game, Mickey went 5-for-5 against a guy named Goat Walker, a knuckleball pitcher with Jacksonville. He also tied for the league lead in errors with 24. And he made a big impression on a local boy with whom he would later cross paths.

"Mickey and I go back farther than even he knows," said former Athletics and Cleveland Indians pitcher Lou Brissie, who was born and raised near Greenville. "I used to go to the park all the time to watch him play. I was about 14. I kind of followed Mickey and Al Brancato. Vernon was unflappable. When he was knocked down, he never reflected that. I think he was an ideal kind of player who really knew his trade and gave his best effort every day."

After the Spinners' season ended, the Senators brought Mickey to Washington to participate in morning workouts at Griffith Stadium. The experience was mostly uneventful except for an incident that happened during a Senators game with the Athletics.

Vernon watched it from a box seat in the stands.

"Buddy Myer was trying to score and he slid in high and spiked the A's catcher, Hal Wagner. It knocked Wagner out, and started a brawl. The players were separated, but the next time Myer came to bat, the A's Bud Thomas knocked his hat off with a pitch. When Myer got to first base, he hollered over to Thomas, 'I don't blame you. You were probably told to do that.'

"Later, Myer came to bat again and singled. When the next batter got a hit, Myer went to third where he slid into the A's Billy Werber, slicing his arm. Werber slammed the ball into Myer's head. Myer was bleeding profusely. And another brawl started. A number of players wound up getting ejected. It was one of the biggest donnybrooks I ever saw."

As he always did, Vernon returned for the winter to Marcus Hook where, until he joined the Navy in 1944, he spent the off-season working at Sun Oil. One year, Mickey worked with the pipe-fitters. Another year, he had a job with the boilermakers. "One year," he said, "I left to work in the barrel house at Sinclair, but they fired me after one month because I wasn't a union member, and I came back to Sun Oil.

"Andy MacMurtrie [an executive at the refinery] always got me jobs at Sun Oil," Vernon said. "And every year when I was a young player he bought me a new glove at Briggs Sporting Goods in Chester. He did that until I got a contract with a glove company after I'd been in the majors for a couple of years."

In the early years of his professional career, Vernon was usually listed in baseball publications as James or Jim. Once, the *Official Baseball Guide*, published by *The Sporting News*, listed him as Jerry. But he was Mickey to most people.

By the time 1939 arrived, Mickey was on the move again. This time when he left Marcus Hook for spring training, he headed for Orlando, Florida, where he would train for the first time with the Washington Senators.

Rookies, of course, got no special treatment from the parent club. And instead of staying in the team's regular hotel in Orlando, they were sent to Ma Simpson's boarding house. Mickey, as well as Early Wynn, Jake Early, Joe Haynes, and about one dozen others lived there and each night competed for food at the dinner table. "I usually got enough to eat because I had the longest reach," Vernon said.

By the time spring training was over, Vernon had been assigned to Springfield (Massachusetts), a Class A team in the

Eastern League. The team had previously been located in Trenton.

At Springfield, Vernon, whose salary had vaulted to $450 per month, roomed with Jimmy Bloodworth and played under manager Spencer Abbott, a colorful, aging, hard-boiled baseball lifer who was as tough as an angry water buffalo.

"He was quite a character," Vernon recalled. "He was a rough old bird. When he'd take a pitcher out, he'd call me and Freddy Chapman to the mound and chew us out instead of the pitcher. He thought we both had big league potential and he wanted to put some life into us.

"Once," Mickey added, "he jumped up in the dugout to holler at somebody and hit his head on the roof. Knocked himself out. The players let him lie there."

The Nationals, as they were called, would finish third in the Eastern League, with a 74-66 record, six games behind the frontrunning Scranton Red Sox. But Mickey wasn't there at the end. Three weeks after Bloodworth was called up to the Senators, Vernon was summoned to Washington, too. The Senators had sent Jimmy Wasdell back to the minors at Minneapolis, and wanted Mickey to take over the first base duties. At the time, he was leading the Eastern League in hitting with a .343 average in 69 games.

"When he went up, Bloodworth had said to me, 'Roomie, I'll have you up there in three weeks.' He did. And it was just a great feeling. Being in the big leagues was what I always wanted. The Senators were not a very good team at the time. But it wouldn't have made any difference what team I was on. I was just glad to be in the big leagues.

"After I got the call to go up," Vernon added, "I didn't tell my parents. I wanted to surprise them. That was the wrong thing to do. My dad should've been there, and he wasn't."

The 21-year-old Vernon had been called by the Senators following a night game in Springfield. He was supposed to be in Philadelphia the next afternoon for a doubleheader against the Athletics, but couldn't get a train. Finally, he arrived at Shibe Park that day in the seventh inning of the first game. On the way to the

At the age of 21, Vernon made his big league debut in 1939.

ballpark, he had stopped at Passon's Sporting Goods store in center city to buy a pair of spikes to replace his beaten and cut old ones.

"When I got to the park, the guy at the gate wouldn't let me in," Vernon said. "They called a guy in the clubhouse, and he came to the gate to identify me. I got dressed and went to the dugout, and in the ninth inning, they put me in as a pinch-runner.

"What a coincidence to play my first game at the park where I'd seen so many games as a kid," Vernon said. "I was really high. What a thrill."

On July 8, 1939—just four days after Lou Gehrig had made his emotional farewell speech at Yankee Stadium—Mickey made his big league debut as a starter in the second game and got his first major league hit, a single off A's pitcher Bill Beckman. That turned out to be his only hit in four trips to the plate.

Vernon, now earning $600 a month, appeared in 76 games with Washington, which at the time was one of the doormats of the American League (the Senators finished sixth in 1939 and seventh in 1940). Mickey hit .257. He hit just one home run, a blast off Johnny Broaca of the Indians on July 22 at League Park in Cleveland. Along the way, he also played against a couple of his boyhood idols.

"Jimmie Foxx and Lefty Grove were with the Boston Red Sox by then," Mickey said. "They, along with Mickey Cochrane, were my idols when they were with the A's. The first time I came up against Grove, my knees were shaking. But I got a hit off him. A single to center.

"He was kind of a mean-tempered guy. When I got to first, he looked over and said, 'Hey, kid, that's the last hit you'll get today.' And it was. Grove wasn't as fast then as he had been, but he had great form, and just watching him was a thrill." The Senators, by the way, lost that game, 22-4.

In his first season in Washington, Vernon also had contact with another Hall of Famer. Former pitcher Walter Johnson was spending his one season as a Senators broadcaster. He called Mickey "James," and often remarked over the air that Vernon was a fine player. Mickey didn't really know Johnson, he said, but would see him when he frequently appeared in the clubhouse to visit Washington manager Bucky Harris.

"My father always had a very high regard for Mickey Vernon," said Johnson's daughter Carolyn Thomas. "He thought he was a gentleman and a fine man."

That winter, the baseball book, *Who's Who in the Major Leagues*, made note of Mickey's arrival. "His fielding was exceptional, and his hitting was slightly less than that," it said. "He could become the regular front door-keeper."

But not yet. Mickey still needed seasoning. "It was a big jump from the Eastern League, and I was overmatched a lot of times," Vernon said. "It's best to start the season with the major league club instead of joining it at mid-season You're better able to prepare yourself."

Nevertheless, he again went to spring training with the Senators in Orlando. By then, other teams were becoming aware of the modest but hard-hitting first baseman with the exceptional glove.

New York Giants manager Bill Terry visited the Washington camp and tried to purchase Vernon. Senators owner Clark Griffith quickly rejected the offer. "You're not going to get him," he said. "He's staying with us." When Cleveland also put in a bid for Mickey, Griffith turned that down, too.

Instead of remaining with the Senators, though, Vernon was sent to the Jersey City Giants of the International League when Washington purchased the well-traveled Zeke Bonura to play first base. The IL was classified as Class AA, which at the time was the highest level in the minors.

The previous year, Jersey City, which had a working agreement with the New York Giants, had won its first pennant in 36 years. The 1940 team, managed by Bert Niehoff, the second baseman on the Phillies' pennant-winning team in 1915, included past or future major leaguers such as Sid Gordon, Dusty Cooke, Herschel Martin, Johnny Dickshot, Glen Stewart, Wayne Ambler, and Woody Jensen.

Jersey City was a rabid baseball city. The team played at Roosevelt Stadium, and on each opening day, the city came to a virtual standstill. Fans flocked to the ballpark and jammed the stands to the rafters. They did likewise during the rest of the season. In 1940, the Giants led the league in attendance with 228,361, nearly 65,000 more than the next highest club (Newark).

"It was a good town to play in, and I enjoyed it very much," Vernon said. "Getting sent down to Jersey City was one of the best things that ever happened to me. I got to play with guys who were either going up or coming down, and that was great experience for a young guy like me. By the time I went back up, I was more than ready."

Vernon, with sportswriters calling him Jimmy, spent the entire season with the Giants, and hit .283 in 154 games. He slugged nine home runs, had 65 RBI, and scored 76 runs. He fielded .989, a career minor league high for him and the fifth best mark among first basemen in the league. And he got beaned by Newark left-hander Tommy Byrne when he stepped into a fastball that he thought was a curve. While not seriously hurt, it was the only time in his career that Vernon was hit in the head by a pitch.

The infield of the Jersey City Giants at the start of the 1940 season consisted of (from left) Mickey Vernon, Sid Gordon, (first name unknown) Roggino, and Glen Stewart.

Jersey City (81-78) finished in third place, 16 games below the first-place Rochester Red Wings. In the Governors' Cup Series after the regular season, the Giants were swept in four games in the first round by the Newark Bears, who went on to win the championship over the Baltimore Orioles.

Following the Giants' elimination, Vernon was recalled by the Senators. He played in five games, hitting .158. But there would be no more minor league games for Mickey. He was in the majors to stay.

CHAPTER 6

In the Majors to Stay

During the long history of major league baseball, few seasons were more remarkable or more memorable than the storied campaign of 1941.

It was the year that Ted Williams hit .406 to become the last major league batter to reach the exalted level of .400. Joe DiMaggio set a still-standing record by hitting in 56 consecutive games. Bob Feller posted his third straight 20-win season, giving him a three-year total of 76 triumphs. Pete Reiser won the National League batting title.

The Brooklyn Dodgers won their first pennant since 1920, but lost to the New York Yankees in a World Series made noteworthy by Mickey Owens' passed ball on a third strike pitch by Hugh Casey with two outs and the Dodgers leading 4-3 in the ninth inning of the fourth game. The blunder allowed Tommy Henrich to reach first base, which set the stage for a Yanks rally and subsequent victory.

It was also the year that Stan Musial made his major league debut. Another rookie named Danny Murtaugh led the National

League in stolen bases with 18. And in Washington, while the Senators' Cecil Travis was leading the league in hits and George Case in stolen bases, Mickey Vernon played his first full season in the big leagues.

For Vernon, 1941 would be one of the most eventful years in his life.

As usual, Vernon had spent the off-season working at Sun Oil. At night, he would hang out with his Marcus Hook pals—Shorty Baldwin, Paul Deary, Harry Edmundson, and others—the group often sitting on a curb eating ice cream or idling around Stesis' news store in the middle of town. As he always did when he lived in Hook, Vernon sometimes had a catch with the neighborhood boys. "It was a big deal to us," said Mickey's younger cousin Al Konegan. "All the kids really admired him."

Mickey had always stayed in shape during the winter. In fact, Vernon's dad, Pinker, once told a reporter, "Mickey doesn't smoke, and he doesn't drink, but he is always in condition."

Some years, Vernon chopped wood. One year when he was in the minors, Mickey's friend, Ted Sheeky, a gravedigger at Lawncroft Cemetery in Linwood, had the young first baseman take down trees to clear spots for graves. "They weren't big trees," recalled Vernon, "so they were pretty easy to take down. I swung the axe right where the strike zone was. I took two swings for each tree, one up, one down." Another year, Vernon went to a woods near Lake Placid, New York, and cut Christmas trees, which he and a friend had shipped to Marcus Hook where they sold them. Once during the off-season, he even got a job on a diary farm milking cows to strengthen his arms.

Around home, Mickey got no special treatment." He didn't get all the attention at home," said his sister Edith Cushman, who is seven years younger than her brother. "Mother and father were very proud of him. My father always got the newspapers from wherever Mickey was playing, and he went to a lot of his games, especially in Washington. But Mickey wasn't favored by my parents."

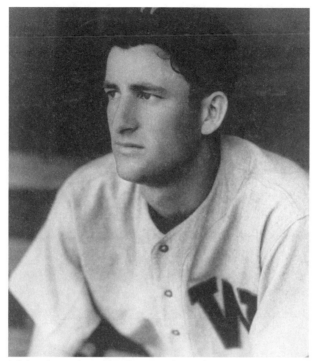

Mickey just missed batting .300 in his first full season in the majors.

Edith herself made no extra fuss over her increasingly prominent brother. A notable brother? "It didn't even dawn on me until I was in high school," she said. "When I was smaller, he just tolerated me. As I became older, the gap closed. But I went to Ridley Park High School instead of Eddystone because I wanted people to like me because of me. I never mentioned that I was Mickey's sister."

In the winter of 1940-41, however, all was not well with Mickey and the Senators. During the off-season, the club had drafted journeyman first baseman George Archie, whose previous big league experience consisted of two at-bats with the Detroit Tigers in 1938. Although Archie had been playing in the Pacific Coast League, his arrival in Washington gave Vernon reason to pause. "I thought, well, I guess I'm going back to the minors," he recalled.

Vernon rejected the contract the Senators sent him. "I wanted $100 more," he said. "I held out and during the hold out, I decided to get married. Then in early March, I got a call from Clark Griffith. 'Get down here,' he said. 'The job's not taken.' I said I was getting married. He said, 'Wait until the season's over.' I told him I was going to get married, and then I would drive down to Florida. So then he was not only trying to talk me out of getting married, but out of driving down."

The girl Mickey planned to marry was Elizabeth Firth. The daughter of Charles and Blanche (Worrell) Firth, she resided in Leiperville (now called Woodlyn) with her family. Elizabeth had been a classmate of Vernon's at Eddystone.

Liz, or Lib as she was also known, played field hockey and basketball at Eddystone. The school yearbook called her "the most popular girl" in the class. "We never dated in high school," Mickey said, "but we danced together sometimes. We started going together after high school."

Mickey and Lib were married on March 14, 1941, in a ceremony at St. Luke's Episcopal Church in Eddystone. Afterward, the couple moved in with her parents with whom they would live for the next 11 years until they bought a house in Wallingford.

Shortly after the wedding, with Mickey having finally signed a contract that would pay him $2,900 for the season, the Vernons headed for Florida. But when they arrived at the Senators' base in Orlando, just as Mickey suspected, the team had installed Archie at first base. During the remaining exhibition season, Vernon played well enough to make the team, but not well enough to unseat Archie at first.

Neverthless, Mickey was confident enough in his chances that he and Lib made a $60 deposit on an apartment across the Potomac River in Virginia. "But right before the first game," Vernon said, "Griffith came up to the batting cage and told me he was going to send me to Minneapolis. I called Lib and said, 'See if we can get our deposit back.' She went over and got it back."

Vernon was still with the club, however, as the season began. Shortly after the home opener, the team went on a road trip. Mickey pinch-hit in a game in Cleveland and slugged a hit. Then he pinch-hit in a game in Detroit and poked another hit. By the time the team reached Chicago, Vernon was in the starting lineup and Archie had been moved to third base. "You're here to stay," manager Bucky Harris told Mickey.

Once he became a regular, the 23-year-old first baseman wasted no time establishing himself as a big league player. And for the rest of the year, he played as one of the up-and-coming stars of the American League.

Vernon was not intimidated. "The league was full of very good players," he said. "With Williams and DiMaggio and Feller, I was in very fast company. But I never experienced the jitters. In fact, everybody told me I was too relaxed. I didn't think so."

In the early 1940s, the Senators didn't exactly tear up the league. In 1941, the team wound up in seventh place, 31 games out of first. But it did have some talent. George Case, Cecil Travis, Buddy Lewis, Doc Cramer, Jimmy Bloodworth, and Jake Early were among the regulars. On the mound, the Nats had the knuckleballer Dutch Leonard, an 18-game winner that season, along with Sid Hudson and Walt Masterson.

Vernon would become lifelong friends with a number of those players, not the least of which was Case, a speedy outfielder from Trenton, New Jersey, who had broken in with Washington in 1937.

"My dad and Mickey were very similar," said George Case Jr. "They were both very modest guys. They had the same values. They were both family men. Their careers were very parallel. And they were very good friends.

"When I was little," Case continued, "Mickey would come to our house all the time. He would hold me on his lap and sing to me. When I got a little older, my friends used to line up at the front door to get his autograph. He always signed for everybody. To me, he was never Mickey Vernon. He was Uncle Mickey. He and Lib were like family."

Uncharacteristically for big league players, Vernon also befriended a batboy. Frankie LaBono was a young teenager who from 1938 to 1941 served as the visiting team's batboy in

Senators manager Bucky Harris was one of Vernon's favorite skippers.

Cleveland. LaBono said that Mickey became almost part of his family, too.

"When the Senators came to town, he often took me to dinner and to a show," LaBono recalled. "Sometimes, he'd come over to my house and my mother would cook a spaghetti dinner. Mickey always brought her a box of candy. What other player would ever do that?"

Another friendship that Vernon developed in those early years was with Walt Masterson, the pitcher from Philadelphia who became Mickey's roommate for eight years.

"When you live in the same house with somebody, you become like brothers," Masterson said. "A special bond forms between roommates. That's what we had.

"But I'll tell you one thing," Masterson added. "Mickey

Vernon holds the record for going to sleep. He's the only man I ever saw who could sit on the side of a bed, remove his socks, and lay down sound asleep. It was a remarkable habit. We always talked in the evening back in the room about that day's game. Then Mickey would lie down and go right to sleep."

There was no sleeping on the diamond, though. Vernon fielded flawlessly—he made only 10 errors all season—and he hit like a veteran. He was on the verge of hitting .300 as the season approached its final weekend.

"We went into New York for a three-game series that would end the season," Vernon remembered. "I was hitting .302. Harris said, 'Do you want to hit .300?' I said, 'Of course, I do.' He said, 'I'll sit you down for the last three games.' I didn't want to do that, so I turned him down.

"After the first two games, my average had dropped below .300," Mickey continued. "Now at Yankee Stadium, the visiting team had to go through the Yankees' dugout to get to its clubhouse. There were more than a few fights after games in that dugout. As I was going through the dugout after the second game, Red Rolfe, the Yankees' third baseman, was sitting there. He said, 'You need a couple of hits tomorrow.' I said, 'Yes, I do.' He said, 'If you get a chance, bunt. I'll play back.'

"I needed two hits to bat .300, but I had only one going into my last at-bat. So I dropped a bunt, but Bill Dickey was catching for the Yankees, and he ran out and picked up the ball and threw me out at first."

Mickey ended the season with a .2994 batting average. Rounded off, it came to .299.

Nearly one-third of Vernon's hits had been for extra bases. Of his 159 safeties, nine were home runs, 27 were doubles, and 11 were triples. Mickey also scored 73 runs and drove in 93. "I felt very good about my first full year," Vernon said.

Most of the season, Vernon batted fifth behind Travis who was second in the league to Williams in hitting with a .359 average while leading the AL in hits with 218. "Every time I looked up,

Cece was either on second or third, and I couldn't avoid knocking him in," Vernon told writers.

Mickey went back to Delaware County, but he didn't stay there long. It was time for another road trip.

"I was hanging around the newspaper store with a couple of guys," said Vernon, "and somebody said, 'Why don't we go see a World Series game?' So we drove up to Brooklyn to see the Dodgers and Yankees at Ebbets Field. We got there about one or two o'clock in the morning. We got in the bleacher line, stood in it all night, and wound up with seats in the upper deck in center field.

"Of course, we had to buy the tickets. When you were in a World Series in those days, you got seven or eight tickets from the club. But you had to pay for them. It was not like it is today where players get 20 or 25 free tickets. Even when I was with the Pirates in 1960, we had to buy tickets. The ones we got were in the upper deck in left field."

Vernon had one other noteworthy post-season experience. This one involved Lib.

"I had to speak at a banquet, and I wasn't used to doing that at the time," Mickey recalled. "Lib went with me, but she was scared that I would mess up. She got so nervous that she was sweating and her dress got soaked. She never went to another banquet until she attended the Delaware County Athletes Hall of Fame banquet in 2004."

By the time spring training rolled around in 1942, the world had changed. United States had entered World War II, and battles were raging in numerous spots around the world. Major league players—like citizens from all other walks of life—were entering the military. And the rosters of big league teams were constantly changing.

For Vernon, another kind of change was brewing. An attempt was being made to have him change his uniform. It was a situation that would be repeated many times during the rest of his career.

Partly because they played in a ballpark tailor-made for left-handed hitters, the Detroit Tigers were attempting to trade first baseman Rudy York and pitcher Bobo Newsom to the Senators for Vernon and Leonard. Griffith squelched the deal in no uncertain terms, although a few months later he acquired Newsom in a straight cash deal.

Having thus retained his position with Washington, Mickey entered the season full of confidence. The same could not be said of the Senators.

Although newcomer Stan Spence hit .323 and Case posted an average of .320, the Senators were largely ineffective and for the third straight year finished in seventh place, this time 39½ games out of first.

That didn't mean they were dull. Not with Big Bobo on the team.

Newsom, sometimes called Buck, was a portly righthander who before his 20-year big league career ended in 1953, would play for eight teams, including the Senators five different times. Newsom, who had a 211-222 career record, was one of the most unforgettable characters in the professional ranks.

"If he was playing today, he'd be outstanding," Vernon said, "because he had so much charisma. They'd love him. He was a showboat, but he had a great relationship with the fans and he had a great arm. He could pitch day after day; once he pitched both ends of a doubleheader.

"He was very superstitious," Vernon added. "He never walked on the foul line. On days he pitched, he drank out of the dugout water fountain standing sideways. And he always picked up papers on the field. One time, Phil Rizzuto tore up some paper into little pieces and dropped them on the mound. Bobo stopped the game while he picked them all up."

Newsom, who wore 00 on his back, once wandered back to the dugout after a wild pitch third strike, then ran out the other side in an attempt to reach first base. He didn't make it. Another time, second baseman Ellis Clary, another one of the team's characters, rented a touring car after a game in St. Louis and took a group of players to an amusement park. Once there, Newsom bought the group

Vernon's first full year in the majors was in 1941.

tickets for a roller coaster ride, but refused to take a ride himself.

"They used to say that whenever Griffith needed a payday, he would buy Bobo back because he would put people in the stands," Vernon said. "Griffith always told Newsom at the beginning of the season, 'I don't care what you do, but don't take any of these young kids out with you.' One time, one of the rookies went out with Bobo, and he took him right down the drain."

Washington played in 151 games in 1942, and Mickey played in every one of them, coming to bat a career-high 621 times. But his average slipped to .271, and he finished with nine home runs again, 86 RBI, and 76 runs. Again, nearly one-third of his hits went for extra bases.

Bucky Harris, who had managed the Senators since 1935 after having also piloted the team as a playing-manager from 1924 to 1928, moved to the skipper's post with the Philadelphia Phillies in 1943. Taking over the Nats, who that spring held training camp at the University of Maryland because of travel restrictions imposed by the war, was former infielder Ossie Bluege, who had played 18 years with the Senators, mostly at third base.

"Harris was a very good manager," Vernon said. "I never heard him raise his voice. He could teach, had good workouts, and players respected him. He had a lot of patience. Bluege was another good one. He was a lot better than he was given credit for being."

One of the new Senators that year was Indian Bob Johnson, who had performed his best baseball in the livery of the Philadelphia Athletics. A long-distance clouter of some note, Johnson had been a fan favorite during his 10 years in Philadelphia. He was also a favorite of Vernon's when Mickey went to Shibe Park as a kid.

Johnson and Vernon quickly became friends. "He was very good to me," Mickey said. "He was a veteran and I was a young guy, but he treated me the way you like people to treat you. After a game early in the season in New York, he came over to me and said, 'Do you have any plans tonight?' I said I didn't. 'Well,' he said, 'you're coming out with me.' We went to a restaurant, and he had the waitress put a pitcher of beer on the table. He said, 'You're going to have a couple of beers. It will loosen you up.' That was the first time I ever tasted beer."

Vernon tasted something else in 1943. It was his first of what would be four inside-the-park home runs. The blow, estimated to have traveled 463 feet to dead center field, came on August 15 with one man on in the seventh inning of the second game of a doubleheader with the Cleveland Indians at Municipal Stadium. It was served by Allie Reynolds and gave Washington and Mickey Haefner a 4-0 victory in a battle of rookie pitchers.

Mickey took part in another memorable event that year. He was present at Yankee Stadium when Babe Ruth batted against

Coach Clyde Milan (right) gave some pointers in 1943 to (from left) Joe Krakauskas, Mickey Vernon, George Case, and Bob Johnson.

Walter Johnson as part of a war bond drive before a crowd of 60,000. "Afterward, I met Ruth in the clubhouse, and got his autograph," Vernon said.

Under Bluege and—like all teams—with a roster further depleted by the war, Washington surged all the way up to second place, finishing 13½ games behind the front-running Yankees. Vernon compiled a .268 batting average with seven home runs, 70 RBI, and 89 runs scored.

He would not, however, see action again in another major league game until 1946.

CHAPTER 7

Anchors Aweigh

It was often said that Washington was first in war, first in peace, and last in the American League. While that slogan might be a slight distortion of the facts, it was not entirely without merit.

The war and peace bit notwithstanding, Washington, a.k.a. the Senators, often finished last in the American League. In fact, that's precisely where they could be found at the end of the 1944 season when a team largely devoid of its best players struggled to the finish line 25 games behind the—of all teams—pennant-winning St. Louis Browns.

By then, World War II had decimated the rosters of all major league teams, leaving the spots to be filled by a jumbled mixture of players too young to join the war effort, too old to serve, or too infirm to be part of the military. Teenagers, graybeards, and 4-Fs, author Harrington (Kit) Crissey called them in his book of the same title on wartime baseball.

The Senators were no exception. They had 41-year-old John Niggeling, 38-year-old Joe Kuhel, 38-year-old Rick Ferrell, 36-year-old Jake Powell, and 35-year-old Dutch Leonard, among others, on the team. They also had an assortment of kids and players ineligible for the draft.

But a number of the club's mainstays were missing from the lineup, including infielder Cecil Travis, outfielder Buddy Lewis, and pitchers Sid Hudson and Walt Masterson. Mickey Vernon, the team's first baseman, had also gone off to war. After three seasons as a regular, the 26-year-old Marcus Hook native had joined the Navy.

Although many others were drafted before him, Vernon's high draft number kept him from entering the armed forces at an earlier date. Mickey didn't receive his draft notice until shortly before the end of the 1943 season. When he did, he asked the local draft board if he could finish the season before getting inducted, and was told he could.

"When I got drafted, I didn't fret about it because everybody else was going in," Vernon said. "I figured that was just the way it was supposed to be. I just tried to make the most of it."

Vernon was inducted on October 13. He reported for processing to an armory in Philadelphia.

"I was standing in line when someone shouted, 'Who wants to go into the Navy?' Vernon told Crissey for his book, *Teenagers, Graybeards, and 4-Fs.* "That sounded okay to me, so I raised my hand. I was directed to a new line where the Navy volunteers were standing.

"I don't know why I chose the Navy," he added. "A week before the season ended, the people with whom my wife and I were living in Washington invited us to go fishing on the Chesapeake Bay. I got so seasick I passed out. But I selected the Navy anyway. And I still got seasick every time I got on a ship."

Vernon spent boot camp at a base in Sampson, New York, in the western part of the state. He then was sent to the naval base at Bainbridge, Maryland, where he trained to become a physical fitness instructor in an eight-week course led by former heavyweight boxing champion Gene Tunney.

Mickey's next stop was Norfolk Naval Air Station where he served part of his time as a fitness instructor connected with the

It was off to the Navy for Mickey in the fall of 1943.

base recreation department. The rest of the time, Vernon played baseball on a team managed by Lt. Herman Franks, who before and after the war was a backup catcher with four teams and later a manager of the San Francisco Giants and Chicago Cubs. The team, which had no major league players of any particular note other than Vernon and Franks, played about 60 games, mostly against local squads and other nearby base teams. Mickey said that he hit about .350.

One of Norfolk's games was against Fort Meade. Joe Cambria, the scout and minor league team owner who had rescued Mickey from the St. Louis Browns, was in the stands.

"I was often accused of not swinging hard enough," Vernon claimed. "Cambria said, 'I'll buy you a new hat if you swing hard.' George Sisler, the son of the Hall of Famer who became a minor league executive and whose brothers Dick and Dave played in the big leagues, was pitching. I took a hard swing, but the pitch broke right into my wrist. Oh, did that hurt. My wrist was very sore. And I never did get the hat."

In October 1944, Vernon and about 30 other players were sent on a converted cargo ship from San Francisco to Honolulu and the base at Pearl Harbor. Mickey was seasick during the entire 11-day trip, and according to Crissey, was too weak to shave, and let his beard grow so long that the other players called him "Abe." Throughout the trip, Vernon had to sleep on the top deck and could hold hardly any food down except ripe olives.

"I was sick before we sailed under the Golden Gate Bridge," Vernon recalled. "I've never been so sick in my life. And you know what? I've never been on a ship since I was in the Navy."

Mickey's job in Honolulu was to help build a baseball field near the barracks. "After about five months in Hawaii, we put together two Navy teams and began working out," Vernon said. "We were told we were going to be shipped to the South Pacific to play exhibition games for the servicemen who were fighting in those areas. We had a lot of big leaguers on those two teams."

Among the big leaguers were pitchers Virgil Trucks, Johnny Vander Meer, Tom Ferrick, Johnny Rigney, Bob Klinger, and Mace Brown; infielders Johnny Mize, Pee Wee Reese, Al Brancato, Pinky May, Johnny Lucadello, Connie Ryan, Elbie Fletcher, Al Glossop, and Buddy Blattner; outfielders Del Ennis, Gene Woodling, Joe Grace, Red McQuillen, and Barney McCosky; and catchers Hal White and George Dickey.

The players were divided into teams representing the Third Fleet and the Fifth Fleet.

Because the power-hitting but slow-footed Mize was on Vernon's Fifth Fleet team and could only play first base, Mickey returned to his old haunt in right field.

"Most of the players on the two teams," Vernon remembered, "were big leaguers except a couple. One was Vinnie Smith. He was a pretty good player in the Pittsburgh Pirates organization who later became a major league umpire [1957-65]. "

Another was Del Ennis, the future Phillies slugger who at the

Players Johnny Mize, Johnny Sain, and Mickey Vernon (from left) from the Navy touring team were greeted by Connie Mack and two of his coaches, Ira Thomas (left) and Chief Bender (right).

time had played just one year of minor league ball at the Class B level. One of the stories recapped by Crissey in *Athletes Away* told how an attempt was made to lure Ennis from the Phillies.

"Ennis looked very good at the plate," Crissey wrote. "His slugging prompted Dan Topping, new owner of the New York Yankees and a fellow serviceman at Pearl, to offer him $25,000 to sign with the Yanks. It was especially tempting because the Phillies had paid him only $50 to sign. But he said, 'I'm already signed,' and that was the end of it."

In February 1945, after several exhibition games in Honolulu, the athletes flew to the South Pacific. There, hopping from island to island in two planes—one on which future Hall of Fame announcer Bob Murphy was the navigator—they played nearly every day for one month. As noted in *Athletes Away*, "Players sat along the sides of the planes with their gear stashed in the middle. Sometimes upon coming into an island, the plane was so heavy that the wheels skimmed the water just before landing.

A team made up mostly of big leaguers made an exhibition tour in the South Pacific in 1944. Among those on the team were Vernon (back, third from left), Barney McCosky, Johnny Mize, Joe Grace, Tom Ferrick (back row), Johnny Vander Meer, Virgil Trucks, Gene Woodling, Del Ennis, Pinky May (middle row), and Hal White, Al Brancato, and Mace Brown (front row).

There were only two parachutes on board each aircraft—for the plane crew only."

The teams played before mostly Marines and sailors in places with strange names such as Guam, Saipan, Peleliu, Kwajalein, Marjuro, Roi, Ulithi, Mog Mog, and Tinian. Altogether, about 25 games were played. In a few cases, explosions could be heard near the ballfields while the games were going on.

Al Brancato, the Philadelphia Athletics' shortstop who was one of the players on the trip, remembered the cumbersome conditions under which the teams worked. "We'd come in, land, play, and then leave to go to the next place," he said. "We were always on the run. You just did what you had to do, but it wasn't always too easy. People thought that because we were big league players, we had it pretty easy. But we didn't. We got no special treatment."

"The games were very intense," recalled Vernon, who hit seven home runs in the first six games. "A big rivalry developed between the teams. It got to be a little bit of a grudge thing. Batters got knocked down. Once, Ryan had a fight with Trucks back in the barracks after a game.

"We usually had crowds of 10-12,000," Vernon added. "But the fields we played on were terrible. Most of them were on land that had been bulldozed by the Seabees. There was no grass. They were often just rock fields. A lot of the fields had pieces of coral on them. Sometimes players got cut by the coral. Some of the fields also had short fences in the outfield. One was about 255 feet away. Batters were hitting balls into the ocean.

"One of the fields we played on," Mickey said, "had been built by the Japanese. It was along the side of a mountain. We were scheduled to play a game there one day, but before the game, some of us went for a ride on a B-29. We got back late, and they had to hold up the game for about an hour. And there were several generals in attendance, plus a crowd of about 15,000 servicemen."

Tennis star Bobby Riggs was part of the baseball contingent. Prior to games, he played exhibition tennis matches with Blattner, an outstanding tennis and ping-pong player. In the evenings, the two played ping-pong games before large crowds.

After the month of touring ended, the teams were disbanded and players were sent back to Guam where they lived in tents with mosquito netting over their cots. Eventually, the men were assigned to bases on a variety of different islands. Some stayed at Guam, some went to Saipan, some went to Tinian. Vernon returned to the small atoll of Ulithi.

There he would stay for the next 10 months.

"The island was part of a horseshoe-shaped area that had 22 atolls," Vernon said. "Prior to going to Iwo Jima, about 800 ships rendezvoused in the channel. Ulithi was not even big enough for a baseball field. It was about one mile long and about one-quarter of a mile wide. Quonset huts covered most of the land."

Vernon was assigned the duties of leading exercises, and running softball and basketball leagues. He officiated at both basketball and softball games, too. One of the players on one of the softball teams was future Boston Red Sox teammate and American League batting champion, Billy Goodman. But Mickey played no baseball during his entire stint on the island.

By then, however, word was starting to sift back to the States about Mickey's feats as a hitter. Eventually, the news reached Senators manager Ossie Bluege. "They can't get the guy out," Bluege was told. "He's the best hitter in the Pacific."

He might have been one of the best judges of talent, too. "The best basketball player and the best softball player in the league," Vernon said, "was a 19-year-old sailor. Many nights, he would stop by my tent, and we would talk or go to a movie together. We became very good friends."

The youth's name was Larry Doby. On his way to the Hall of Fame, Doby played in the Negro League for the Newark Eagles, and Vernon would send him bats. Later, the two became teammates with the Cleveland Indians. And they remained good friends for all the years after their playing days ended. Indeed, several months after Doby died, his daughter Chrissie attended the luncheon and unveiling of Vernon's statue.

"The name Mickey Vernon has been in my house since I was a little kid," said Larry Doby Jr. "My father thought the world of Mickey. He was a genuine, real guy, and my father always spoke highly of him.

"Mickey was always very supportive of my father," Doby added. "He thought he deserved a chance to play professional baseball. In fact, one time he wrote a letter to Clark Griffith asking him to give my father a tryout. Even after my father became the first African-American player in the American League and was not treated well by many of the others, Mickey Vernon always stood up for him.

"When they named a field in Patterson, New Jersey, after my father, Mickey came to the dedication. That was in 2001, two years before my father died. He was just so pleased that Mickey came and took part in the event."

Eventually, Vernon reached the rank of first class petty officer. In the fall of 1945, with the war finally over, he was sent to San Francisco and in December he received his discharge.

Mickey was supposed to travel by train back to the East Coast, but he elected to fly so he could get home faster. He arrived in New York on December 26. Soon he would start to get ready for a long-awaited new baseball season. It would be a season that ranked as one of the most memorable in Vernon's career.

CHAPTER 8

Beating the Mighty Williams

The year was 1946. It was a special time in America.

Peace, sweet peace, had been restored. World War II and all of its horrors had finally ended. The boys had returned home from all those faraway places with the strange names, and the nation was making a valiant attempt to get back to normal.

There were, of course, a great many repairs to make, both socially and otherwise. But for the most part, Americans were buoyed by a sense of exuberance that had long been missing. For many citizens, life was fun again. It was an exciting time.

Nowhere was this more true than in baseball. Rosters brimmed with players who had returned from the war. All the big names were back, and the teams had been restored to their full strengths. And Americans flocked to ballparks in record numbers.

In the American League, much of the attention focused on returning sluggers Ted Williams and Joe DiMaggio. Each one had missed at least three full seasons of baseball. The 1941 season—when Williams had hit .406 and DiMaggio had hit in 56 straight games—was still fresh in people's minds. Although five years had passed, it was assumed that the two would renew their fight for supremacy as the league's premier batter.

No one figured that that supremacy would be contested by a guy named Mickey Vernon. After all, the quiet, slender first baseman of the Washington Senators was not regarded as one of the league's top hitters; indeed, he had never even hit .300 in three previous seasons as a regular. And having just returned himself from two years of military service, he hadn't played a lick of competitive ball in all of 1945.

Who in the world would be so bold as to suggest that the 28-year-old Vernon would be a major part of the American League's 1946 batting equation? That view was reflected in the salary Washington owner Clark Griffith paid Vernon. It was $9,000 for the year.

In the previous three years, with the rosters of all teams changing constantly, the Senators had gone from second place to last place and back to second place. The 1946 team included well-established position players such as Cecil Travis, Buddy Lewis, Stan Spence, and Gerry Priddy, and a strong pitching staff that included veterans Dutch Leonard, Bobo Newsom, Ray Scarborough, Sid Hudson, and Early Wynn.

Vernon had spent the winter preparing for the upcoming season by working out every day and playing handball at the Chester YMCA with his pal Danny Murtaugh, a practice they did nearly every off-season after the war. Mickey also bulked up, and he came to spring training weighing close to 200 pounds. The added poundage figured to give Vernon some extra pop in his bat.

When the season began, Mickey was ready. He laced three hits in the season's opener on April 16 at Griffith Stadium against the Boston Red Sox. Strangely, manager Ossie Bluege, who claimed he would not play Mickey against some lefthanded pitchers, benched Vernon for the third and fourth games of the season, replacing him with somebody named Jack Sanford. But then Mickey returned to the lineup in the fifth game and stayed there the rest of the way.

From that point on, Vernon found himself fighting Williams for the league lead in hitting. The Boston Red Sox slugger had won the AL batting title in 1941 and 1942, but then spent the next three years in the service where he became a Marine fighter pilot. Although he saw no action in combat, Williams had played in a number of baseball games in 1945 in Hawaii in a league with many major league players.

There were no water fountains, so Mickey grabbed a quick drink from a hydrant at spring training in 1946 at Orlando, Florida.

Ted was ready for the 1946 season, too. And in the season opener at Griffith Stadium with President Harry S. Truman and General Dwight D. Eisenhower in the stands, Williams showed just how ready he was. On the first pitch thrown to him, Williams blasted a drive into the 12th row of the left-center field bleachers, some 418 feet from home plate. It was said to be the longest drive ever hit into that section.

Williams continued to pepper the ball, and bolstered by three straight three-hit games, he was hitting a lofty .424 by May 9. Meanwhile, Vernon, who on the same date was batting .415, had begun a 22-game hitting streak on April 30 during which he would pound 40 hits in 98 trips to the plate. Four times during the streak, Mickey got three hits in one game. Once he got four. That day, Vernon would later say, "was the best day of my career."

It came on May 19, when the Senators met the Chicago White Sox in a doubleheader at Comiskey Park. Vernon hit a home run and a double off Ted Lyons in the first game, which was won 4-3

A frequent visitor to Griffith Stadium in 1946 and a fan of Vernon's was Capt. Ted Lawson who lost a leg after getting shot down while piloting a B-29 over Japan. One of Jimmie Doolittle's flyers, Lawson later wrote the book *30 Seconds Over Tokyo*, which was later turned into a movie.

by the Chisox. In the second game, Mickey hit for the cycle off Eddie Lopat in a 7-1 victory for Washington and John Niggeling.

In an unusual twist for cycles, Vernon needed a single in his last at-bat. He got it. "It was a clean shot," Mickey recalled. "All four hits were clean hits."

Vernon wound up going 6-for-8 in the doubleheader against two of the top pitchers in the American League. "I have nothing but respect for that fellow," Lopat said.

By the end of the streak on May 27, Vernon was hitting .405 with 45 hits in 111 trips to the plate. Williams, who had tailed off, was hitting .351. Ted, however, heated up again, and by the end of June, he was hitting .358. At the same time, Vernon, having tailed off himself despite a 10-game hitting streak at the start of the month, had dropped to .355.

As July began, the All-Star Game was approaching. There had been no game in 1945 because of wartime travel restrictions, so the 1946 contest to be held at Boston's Fenway Park was anxiously awaited. When the final votes were counted, both Vernon and Williams had won starting berths on the team.

"Being chosen for the squad is the biggest thrill I've ever had in baseball," Vernon told reporters.

In his two trips to the plate, Mickey grounded out against National League starter Claude Passeau of the Chicago Cubs and flied out against Kirby Higbe of the Brooklyn Dodgers. Perhaps somewhat ironically, both hurlers were former moundsmen with one of Vernon's hometown teams, the Philadelphia Phillies.

Williams, meanwhile, had the finest All-Star Game of his lengthy career. Slamming four hits, he blasted a fourth inning home run into the center field bleachers off Higbe, then in the eighth sent a blooper pitch by the Pittsburgh Pirates' Rip Sewell into the right field bullpen. Paced by Williams' five RBI, the American League captured a lopsided 12-0 victory.

Soon afterward, it was back to the regular season. Two days after the All-Star break, Vernon lashed three hits. Then he got four hits in a game on July 19 and four more on July 25. On July 28, Vernon hit his second inside-the-park home run of the season, this one coming off Allie Reynolds and the Cleveland Indians (Mickey's second homer of this kind off Reynolds). A little less than two months earlier, he had hit one off Fred Hutchinson and the Detroit Tigers.

By the end of the month, Mickey was hitting .357, but he was sufficiently unhappy with his salary that he marched into Griffith's office and demanded an increase. Naturally, he didn't get it. Meanwhile, Williams, also buoyed by two four-hit games— one that included three home runs against the Cleveland Indians—carried a .355 average.

Years later, Vernon admitted he was in awe of the Red Sox slugger. "I'd stand by the batting cage just to watch him hit," he said. "I would tell him, 'Ted, it embarrasses me to think that I'm ahead of you. I'm not really in the same class.' But it was a terrific feeling being in a race with such a great hitter."

Vernon might have held Williams in the highest regard, but

Mickey's friend Sid Stesis (right) was chairman of the committee when the people of Marcus Hook honored the Washington slugger and wife Lib in 1946 at Shibe Park.

there were others who felt the same way about him. They were Mickey's friends and relatives from Delaware County where he grew up.

On August 9, they declared Mickey Vernon Day in Delaware County. Tributes came in from two governors—Edward Martin of Pennsylvania and Walter Bacon of Delaware—as well as from Connie Mack, Clark Griffith, J. Taylor Spink, publisher of *The Sporting News*, and many others.

Typical of the comments was the one from White Sox pitcher Johnny Rigney. "In my book," he wrote, "Mickey Vernon is one of the best hitters in the American League." Philadelphia Athletics first baseman George McQuinn said: "I have come to know him as one of the finest and most sincere people in the league." And Spink claimed that "baseball can never have enough Mickey Vernons."

The batting race continued at a torrid pace through August. Leading throughout the month, Mickey's average in mid-August soared to .349. Despite going just 2-for-19 at one point, Vernon clung to the lead at the end of the month with a .339 average. Williams finished August at .335.

"The hits were just flying off the bat," Vernon remembered. "I was getting lots of hits to left field. I was not a pull hitter like Williams. If I bunted the ball, it would roll halfway down the line and stop dead, just where no one could field it. If I was fooled on a pitch and swung late, the ball would sail just over the infield and just short of the outfield. Everything clicked. And I was in good shape, too."

"He was dangerous any time he stepped to the plate with that classic swing and confident manner," said Shirley Povich of the Washington *Post*.

Vernon's achievements were particularly commendable in view of the fact that he was a lefthanded batter in a predominantly left-handed-hitting lineup that was often compelled to face lefthanded pitchers. "He doesn't get much of a break," wrote Povich. In addition, Vernon was getting a lot of "leg hits," beating out bunts and infield grounders with his speed. Over a two-game stretch at one point, Mickey dropped four bunt singles. It was calculated that his speed produced at least 20 leg hits during the season.

Vernon began September with a 15-game hitting streak. By the end of that spurt, he was carrying a .354 average. At the same time, Williams was at .443. With the season ending on September 29, it all came down to the last two weeks of the campaign.

As it did, the Red Sox, managed by Clark Griffith's son-in-law Joe Cronin, were running away with the American League pennant, and would eventually finish 12 games ahead of the second place Detroit Tigers and capture their first flag since 1918. Griffith's Senators, skippered by former Washington star Ossie Bluege and on their way to going over one million in attendance for the only time in club history, were fighting for a spot in the first division in what would turn out to be a fourth-place finish.

During the final month of the season, the Athletics' right fielder Elmer Valo had suddenly thrust himself into the batting race. It wasn't with the bat. It was with the glove.

In a four-game series between the A's and Red Sox in Boston, Valo had made sparkling catches that took home runs away from Williams in each of the four games. Then two weeks later, the A's and Bosox again met at Fenway Park. In the first game, Valo made a running catch, racing with his back to the plate, of another Williams smash that was headed for home run territory. Then in the second game, he made a leaping grab to rob Williams of another homer. Later in the same game, Elmer crashed into the wall while making another leaping catch of a Williams home run bid. Valo thudded to the ground, but held onto the ball and was shortly thereafter carried off the field on a stretcher.

Vernon came down the stretch like a runaway freight train. One game after his 15-game streak ended, he went on a 9-for-17 tear that included two three-hit games. Mickey was up to .357. Williams, however, had started to fade. And entering the final weekend of the season, he had gone just 4-for-17 and was hitting .340.

When the two sluggers met late in the season, Williams greeted Vernon with a "Hi, champ." "There's still a week to go," Vernon replied. "Ah," said Williams, "you're in and you know it."

Vernon went 4-for-15 in the last three games of the season to finish at .353. Williams got four hits in eight at-bats to wind up with a .342 average. Boston's Johnny Pesky finished third at .335, followed by George Kell of the Tigers at .322, and Dom DiMaggio of the Red Sox with a .316 mark.

For Vernon, his batting crown made him only the fourth player who'd ever won a batting title in a Washington uniform. Ed Delahanty in 1903, Goose Goslin in 1928, and Buddy Myer in 1935 were the only others.

"Because this was my first batting title, it was more satisfying than the second one," Vernon said. "But there was a lot of pressure. When a fellow who's as great a hitter as Ted Williams is breathing down your neck all season, it really puts the pressure on you."

Vernon finished with a career-high 207 hits, placing one behind the league-leading Pesky. Fifty-one of Mickey's hits were doubles, which led the circuit.

Mickey Vernon and Stan Musial were batting champions of their respective leagues in 1946.

"We were playing the Senators in the last game of the season," remembered Pesky, "and Earl Johnson was pitching for us. He said to me, 'Do you want me to pitch to Vernon?' He was trying to make sure I would end up with the most hits. I said, 'Absolutely, you pitch to him. If he gets a hit and wins, I'll be glad to give it to him. Mickey was a class guy, a real gentleman, and he was a great hitter. I wouldn't have minded if a guy like that had beaten me out."

Vernon also hit eight home runs, drove in 85, and scored 88. He had 13 three-hit games and four four-hit games. He failed to get a hit in just 27 games.

With 38 home runs and 123 RBI, Williams finished second to the Tigers' Hank Greenberg in both categories. He led the AL in runs (142), total bases (343), and slugging average (.667). Ted, who would win batting titles in each of the next two years, was named the league's Most Valuable Player with 224 votes. Vernon finished fifth with 134 votes.

Having just spent two years in the service and then gone through a pressure-packed race for the batting crown, one might have thought Vernon would go home after the season for a long winter's nap. But that was hardly the case. Mickey still had more games to play. Thirty-five of them to be exact.

"At the All-Star Game in Boston, Bob Feller had talked to me about going on a barnstorming trip after the season," Vernon recalled. "The idea was that a team of major league all-stars would most of the time play a team of all-stars from the Negro League. He asked me if I'd like to go, and I said, 'Sure.' He said if I still led the league in hitting at the end of the year, he'd give me a bonus."

Although barnstorming after the regular season was a popular activity for professional baseball players anxious to make a little extra money, and for fans, especially those who had never seen big league players perform, trips had been limited to 10 games. To play more than that, Feller had to get special permission from baseball commissioner and former U. S. Senator Albert B. (Happy) Chandler.

Chandler agreed on one condition. Feller, who according to an article in the *Saturday Evening Post*, had incorporated and stood to make upwards of $100,000 on the trip, had to play a game in the commissioner's hometown of Versailles, Kentucky. Feller, of course, quickly consented.

"The game was played on a high school field," Vernon remembered. "Afterward, the players all went back to Chandler's house for a dinner and party. Then we had to leave to play another game that night in Cincinnati."

In addition to Vernon, Feller's all-stars included players such as Stan Musial, Phil Rizzuto, Charlie Keller, Ken Keltner, Sam Chapman, Jim Hegan, Jeff Heath, Johnny Berardino, and Frankie Hayes, and pitchers Johnny Sain, Warren Spahn, Dutch Leonard, Spud Chandler, and Bob Lemon, who was just making the switch from third base to the mound. Among Negro League players were Buck O'Neill, Quincy Trouppe, Gene Benson, Hank Thompson,

Artie Wilson, and Hilton Smith. Comedian Jackie Price accompanied the team and entertained fans before each game.

Over a 27-day period, the teams played 35 games, including 11 doubleheaders, only one with both games played in the same city. Each team traveled on a charter bus, although sometimes they flew long distances on two chartered planes. Big league players were paid salaries ranging from $1,700 to $6,000 for the tour with Negro Leaguers making much less.

"One time," Vernon recalled, "we played an afternoon game in Newark [New Jersey] and in Baltimore that night. Another time, we played in New Haven in the afternoon and in Yankee Stadium at night. We went all across the country. We played in Crosley Field in Cincinnati, League Park in Cleveland, Comiskey Park in Chicago. We ended up in California. The tour drew well over one-quarter of a million people."

When their respective teams met, Feller, who missed only two games, and Paige each pitched the first two or three innings. The ageless Paige impressed all of his Caucasian opponents, some of whom had never seen him pitch before.

"I firmly believe that if he'd been in the major leagues starting in his early 20s," Vernon said, "they'd still be shooting at some of his records. He had slowed down by then, but he could still pitch. He had great control. Later on when he was with Cleveland, he was warming up and Hegan was catching. They put a chewing gum wrapper in front of Hegan and Paige threw 8 or 10 pitches right over it. He didn't have much of a breaking ball, but he was very fast.

"The Negro League team had some pretty good players," Vernon added. "One was a spitball pitcher named White, and he was getting us out. The batters complained. Feller talked to Satchel and they sent him home. 'Well fellows, you won't have to play against him anymore,' Paige said."

During the tour while the team was on the West Coast, Vernon threatened to go home, claiming he had been away too long and missed his wife and family. Furthermore, it was Lib's birthday, and he wanted to be there. Feller solved the problem by flying Lib to California.

Flying then, as now, could sometimes get rather frightening. Such was the case as the teams began a flight from San Diego to Los Angeles. Shortly after takeoff, the plane lost one of its engines and began losing altitude.

"Lib and I were sitting behind Feller," Vernon recalled. "Across the aisle was Sam Chapman and Johnny Sain. All three had been pilots in the war and knew what was going on. We were told that the plane had to return to San Diego. We flew back through fog along the coast, going about 70 miles per hour. It couldn't have been any scarier."

When the tour finally ended in LA, the team had a gala party at Slapsie Maxie's, a popular nightclub and celebrity hangout. Brooklyn Dodgers manager Leo Durocher was there with his wife, actress Laraine Day. So was actor George Raft, who sent a car the next day to chauffeur Mickey and Lib around the town.

After the 13,000-mile tour ended, Feller had one more present for Vernon. True to his word, the pitcher gave Mickey the $750 bonus he had promised back in July. The money was a fitting climax to what had been a truly remarkable season.

The Two-Year Slump

Mickey Vernon entered 1947 with a new title and a new image. He was a Batting Champion. And he was now viewed as one of the premier hitters in the American League.

He had gained a new level of respect. His name had become familiar. He was in demand. He was now perceived as a member of baseball's upper crust.

For a guy who had been known for his modesty and his unwillingness to stand in the spotlight, this was a major transition. Where once Vernon was a quiet, unassuming player who sought neither fame nor glory, he now had to contend with vastly expanded amounts of attention. It was a whole new ballgame for the guy with the simple tastes from Marcus Hook.

At the front office level, Vernon would be a constant source of trade rumors. He would eventually be swapped from Washington and then come back. Mickey would regularly become a holdout in the off-season, always to the considerable consternation of Senators' owner Clark Griffith. His batting average would fluctuate, and

Taking an off-season break, Mickey relaxed at home after winning the American League batting title.

when it dipped, he would get a glimpse of the unpleasant side of baseball.

All the while, his demeanor never changed. "Vernon's greatest quality is his deportment on and off the field," wrote columnist Bob Addie in the Washington *Post*. "A quiet, well-behaved athlete who has no vices, he makes that worn-out phrase brand new: A credit to the game."

As they always did, Vernon's teammates and his opponents had equally good things to say about the way he played. One of them was Eddie Yost, the Senators' third baseman and a fixture in Washington from 1947 through 1958.

"If you watched him for any length of time, you understood how good he was," Yost said. "He was one of the best first basemen I ever played with or against. He was a wonderful ballplayer. He hustled all the time. He was very consistent. He was just excellent in so many different ways. And he was never a showboat."

Eddie Joost was on the other side of the field, first as a shortstop with the Philadelphia Athletics, then as the team's last manager before it moved to Kansas City. "I could never say anything that is not the best about him," Joost said. "All the years I was in the American League, he was always recognized as a helluva ballplayer and a great person.

"He was a tough hitter," Joost added. "He was not easy to strike out. He had great ability to field the ball. He had no real weaknesses. The way he played first base, the way he hit, the way he handled himself, he was just a great all-around player. Right at the top. He was as good as anybody in the league, and if you'd talk to other people, they would say the same thing. He just went out and did his job and did it well."

Another player on the other side of the field who admired Vernon was center fielder Dom DiMaggio of the Boston Red Sox. "He was a fine ballplayer," DiMaggio said. "He wasn't what you'd call a flashy guy and he did everything so easily without seeming to strain. But he was an excellent competitor. He drove hard every day. He was just a steady, grind-it-out kind of guy, and he produced. And that's what counted."

Nobody realized this more than the ownership of the New York Yankees. Starting in 1947, the club made what was almost an annual bid for Vernon's services. And it didn't hold back. Money or players to trade were never problems for the Yanks.

In January 1947, Yankees general manager Larry MacPhail told sportswriters that he was willing to pay the then-exorbitant sum of $150,000 for Vernon. MacPhail claimed that if that didn't work, he'd give the Nats first baseman Nick Etten, third baseman Bill Johnson, and outfielder Johnny Lindell—all starters at one time or another—plus cash for Vernon. At one point, he also said he would include relief pitcher Joe Page in the deal in place of one of the other players.

"I've swapped only one star in my life," responded Griffith, "and that was Joe Cronin, my son-in-law. I traded him [to the Boston Red Sox] because he was in the family. But there isn't enough money in that bush league town of New York to buy Mickey Vernon. Vernon will play first base for the Washington Senators next season or not at all. They can offer a million dollars and Vernon will still play for Washington. I'm not going to sell him, and I'm not going to trade him. If I let him go, they'd run me out of town."

The Yankees, however, were persistent. At one point, they reportedly offered the fabled Joe DiMaggio for Vernon in a straight trade. Mickey had always admired the great New York slugger.

"He was a very quiet guy," Vernon said. "He seldom said much to you. A lot of times when a guy would get to first base, I'd say something to him. When DiMaggio broke George Sisler's American League record for hitting in the most consecutive games, it was against Washington. When he got to first base, I said something like, 'Nice going. Congratulations.' He barely acknowledged it. Most of the time, though, we'd chat a little."

Mickey certainly wouldn't have minded going to the Yankees. "There was always some kind of rumor about my going to New York," he said. "That would've been fine with me. Detroit was always trying to get me, too. Both teams had good parks to hit in. It was good to know somebody else wanted me."

Some writers speculated that the real reason Griffith wouldn't deal Vernon to the Yankees was because of his intense dislike for MacPhail. But Griffith may have thought about reversing his position a short time later after Mickey presented his salary demand.

Having been paid just $9,000 the year before, Vernon told Griffith he wanted $25,000. Griffith scoffed, and, claiming the demand was absurd, told reporters, "He never hit .300 in his life before last season." Why then, he reasoned, should he pay that kind of money?

"If I don't get good money after a good year," Vernon was quoted as saying, "I'm certainly not going to get it after a bad one."

Over the years, Vernon and the foxy owner had endured a strange relationship. Sometimes it was up. Sometimes it was down. The previous year, the bat manufacturer Hillerich & Bradsby had given Mickey $500 for winning the batting title (the company later replaced the cash award with a silver bat). Griffith had said publicly that he gave Vernon a $5,000 bonus when in fact he had really given him a $500 war bond.

After one of his many salary squabbles, Vernon signed a contract in 1947 with Senators' owner Clark Griffith.

"I really liked him, despite our battles," Vernon said. "He was a very good person except at contract time. He smoked those long cigars, and juice would run down his face. He'd look at you with those big bushy eyebrows. He was quite a character.

"But he always tried to cut your salary if you had a bad year. And even if you didn't, you always had to fight for a raise. He was tough to deal with.

"One time, Lib was coming north from spring training on a train," Vernon added. "She was by herself. Griffith, who was then about 80, walked through seven cars to find her and invite her to dinner with him. He didn't want her to eat alone."

The Nats' owner, though, was a tough sell. Or as Shirley Povich editorialized in the Washington *Post*, "Mickey Vernon happens to be playing for one of the two cheapest owners in the major leagues." The other, of course, was the Philadelphia Athletics' Connie Mack.

Griffith finally relented and gave Vernon a raise for the 1947 season. Although it was not quite what Mickey wanted, the $20,000 he got was considerably better than his salary the previous year. Besides, Vernon had just signed a contract with Wheaties that would put a few more dollars in his pocket.

Vernon, who Washington manager Ossie Bluege described as "a good boy," was determined to prove that the 1946 season was no fluke, as some had called it. And he went to spring training with high expectations for the season, even though he remained in the shadow of Ted Williams. "I've got the fever and I expect to keep it," he told Oscar Fraley of *United Press International.* "Certainly, I'd like to win the batting championship again, but that Williams is a terrific hitter."

Vernon told Fraley that if Williams learned to hit to left field, he'd raise his batting average by 20 points. Mickey, meanwhile, was already a practitioner of that art, a tactic that worked well in keeping rival defenses off balance.

At spring training, several baseball writers were loitering under the sun when a discussion arose over who was the best first baseman in the American League. "You spell it Y-o-r-k," a scribe from Chicago said. "You have it all wrong," responded a New York essayist. "It should be spelled Mc-Q-u-i-n-n." To which a Washington typewriter jockey blurted, "And it's pronounced Mickey Vernon."

When asked if he really thought he could repeat his perform-ance of the previous year, Vernon had an answer. "They still have to outhit me," he said. "I'm not going to resign. But all I'm really interested in is getting the most hits and trying to win some games for our club."

But something was missing. Mickey floundered once the sea-son got underway. And he continued to have problems with the bat as the campaign progressed.

"He's been chasing bad balls, taking called strikes, fiddling with his stance and grip, and getting an inordinate number of line drives caught when he did meet the ball well," analyzed Povich. "Last year, he was dangerous any time he stepped to the plate. This year, there's been a seepage somewhere."

Griffith, of course, had his theories, too. "He's got to forget about trying to place his hits like he was doing last year to get that big batting average, " the old former pitcher said. "A fellow in that kind of slump ought to be glad to meet the ball instead of trying to be cute about where he hits it. He should lay back and try to knock everything into right field."

Along with his trouble at the plate, Vernon had to deal with another problem. He was being criticized for what some people were saying was his easy-going manner. Bluege, who was already on the hot seat and had been the subject of angry complaints by some of his players, even went so far as to contact Mickey's father and ask him what could be done "to build a fire under the boy." Pinker's response was short and to the point. "He's always been quiet," he said.

Nevertheless, Vernon's batting average plummeted 88 points. While playing in all of the Senators' 154 games, he finished the season with a .265 average with just seven home runs. His doubles total dropped from 51 to 29, but he scored 77 runs and drove in 85.

"It was the worst slump of my career," Vernon said. "Everybody was asking the reason, but I couldn't put a finger on it. I thought I was hitting just as well, but I wasn't getting the hits. I go along with what Williams said. He said one of the toughest things in sports is hitting a baseball. But I would add to that, one of the toughest things in sports is hitting a baseball safely.

"I think my problem was more than bad luck. I was hitting the ball pretty sharply, but you can hit it hard and not do a thing if you're unlucky enough to hit it at somebody. But they were also playing me a little differently—more straightaway—and the pitchers may have found out a little something about me. After the previous year, they were certainly pitching me a lot more carefully."

Williams ran away with the batting title, hitting .343 to beat Barney McCosky of the Athletics by 15 points. And the Senators, with a total of just 42 home runs for the year, finished a dismal season in seventh place, 33 games out of first. Their only consolation was that the St. Louis Browns were even worse.

The era was one in which the Senators typically finished seventh or eighth. "By July, they're thumbing through hunting magazines and travel guides," someone said. "The fellows know that they have no chance." Added third baseman Eddie Yost: "The team just didn't play the caliber of ball that would get us out of the second division. We were never really very strong down the middle, and that's what you have to be to have a winner."

As he always did, Vernon returned to Delaware County for the off-season. While he and Lib continued to reside with her parents in Leiperville, Mickey was a familiar figure in Marcus Hook. One of the places where he could often be found was at Stesis' News Store. Before it was sold in the 1970s, the store had been operated by the Stesis family for more than 50 years. Sid Stesis and his wife Florence had taken over the store from Sid's parents in the 1940s.

"Marcus Hook was a big sports town, and a lot of sports people hung out at the store," recalled Florence Stesis. "When he came home, Mickey was always there. He and the others gathered at the store and talked sports. Sid always had games on the radio. But people would come to the store just to see Mickey. And they'd follow him around like little poodles. Sometimes, if he'd had a big game and came home, they'd drive him around Marcus Hook and Chester. He was very quiet, but he always had a smile on his face and he was always concerned about other people."

Chubby Imburgia, whose family resided across from the Vernon house on Green Street, also remembered Mickey's visits to his hometown. "He'd come over and sit on the porch and talk," said Imburgia, a teenager at the time. "He'd walk around town and talk to everybody. Often, people wanted his autograph, and he'd stand there and sign for anybody who'd ask. If there was a game going on, he'd stop and watch the kids play. Sometimes, he'd even bring other players from the Senators home with him."

Although it mattered little to Mickey's friends in Marcus Hook, his troubles at the plate were not confined to the 1947 season. But his problems extended beyond mere batting averages.

Adversaries for the batting title the previous year, Ted Williams and Mickey Vernon got together during the 1947 season.

Joe Kuhel had replaced Bluege, who had served five years as Senators' manager. A veteran of 18 big league seasons, Kuhel was the middleman in a chain of three great Washington first basemen that had begun with Joe Judge in 1916 and continued on through Vernon. Kuhel had been in the big leagues since 1930 when he broke in with Washington. Later, he spent six seasons with the Chicago White Sox before returning to the Senators in 1944.

Kuhel was not one of the team's most popular managers. "I didn't get along with him," Vernon said. "I don't know exactly why. It was nothing personal. We just didn't seem to hit it off."

The manager's unpopularity may have been reflected in another one of the Senators' poor finishes. Again, they finished seventh, but this time with 97 losses and 40 games out of first. Only a 101-loss season by the Chicago White Sox kept Washington from total embarrassment.

Although he was selected for the American League team in the All-Star Game—and walked and scored as a pinch-hitter for Walt Masterson in his only trip to the plate—Vernon's numbers tumbled again in 1948. While Williams was winning his second straight batting crown with a .369 average—14 points higher than the Cleveland Indians' playing-manager Lou Boudreau—Mickey finished with a .242 mark, a career low as a regular. Although playing in 150 games, Mickey hit just three home runs and collected only 48 RBI.

"There was nothing wrong with me," Vernon recalled. "I just didn't hit."

The fans were not kind. Nor was the press. "He looked lazy and lackadaisical," said one report in *The Sporting News.*

Vernon, though, had his allies. None was a stronger supporter than pitcher Sid Hudson.

Along with pitchers Masterson and Ray Scarborough, Hudson was one of Mickey's best friends on the Senators. The four players and their wives were also close friends socially.

"He had some tough times, but he never let it show," said Hudson. "He was a real professional. Sometimes, if I was in trouble on the mound, he'd come over and talk to me, try to settle me down. You'd never know he was in a slump. As a pitcher, you were darn glad to have him there. "

During the 1948 World Series, another trade rumor involving Vernon circulated through baseball's inner circles. Mickey was going to be swapped to the Boston Red Sox for infielder Johnny Pesky.

It didn't happen. Nor did a rumored swap with the Detroit Tigers. But on December 14, a trade was made. Washington shipped Vernon and pitcher Early Wynn to the Indians for pitchers Joe Haynes and Ed Klieman and first baseman Eddie Robinson. And just like that, more than one decade in the Senators' organization had ended for Vernon.

Haynes, who had originally played with the Senators, had married into the Griffith family. Both he and Klieman were pitchers of no particular note. Robinson was a burly power-hitter of respectable ability, but not close to Vernon's level as a fielder. Most analysts viewed the trade as a disaster for Washington.

"Wynn and I had both had bad years," Vernon said. "Neither of us got along with Kuhel. Griffith wanted to get rid of us. The fans were really riding me, and I wanted to get out of Washington. I was glad to go. I was going to a lot better club. They had just won the World Series, and I thought they had a chance to do it again."

The Yankees had also put in one of their frequent bids for Vernon. But Cleveland, which two months earlier had defeated the Red Sox in a one-game playoff for the American League pennant, then beaten the Boston Braves in six games in the World Series, had wanted Mickey more.

Boudreau observed: "We're getting an established big league ballplayer and one of the best defensive first basemen in the business. Robbie was a fine fielder, but Vernon will cover more ground, and he'll start more force plays and double plays, if only because he's lefthanded. When I decided we might have to give up Robinson in a trade, I made it a point to ask [owner] Bill Veeck not to give him up unless we got another good first baseman."

They got not only that, but the Indians also landed a pitcher who would someday reside in the Hall of Fame. For both players—later Indians roommates—the deal liberated them from the dregs of the American League and the continuous frustration that accompanies those who perform with a losing team. And it offered a fresh start that was more than welcome.

CHAPTER 10

Out and Back

After an association that extended back to 1938, Mickey Vernon was no longer part of the Washington Senators organization. It was a strange feeling, but it was not without benefits.

In getting traded to the Cleveland Indians, Vernon was instantly elevated to the elite levels of the American League. As the defending World Champions, the Indians presided over a five-team conglomerate that with the Boston Red Sox, New York Yankees, Philadelphia Athletics, and Detroit Tigers posed a formidable body that dominated the league.

The Senators were definitely not part of that group. And in dumping the W that had flapped for so many years on his chest, Vernon had in a very real sense experienced the kind of liberation that comes when one escapes from the chains of bondage—in this case, the lowly Senators.

After rejecting offers for Vernon for many years, often saying he would never deal away his star first baseman, Washington owner Clark Griffith had suddenly assumed a conciliatory tone in explaining his new-found motives. "I traded Mickey Vernon for

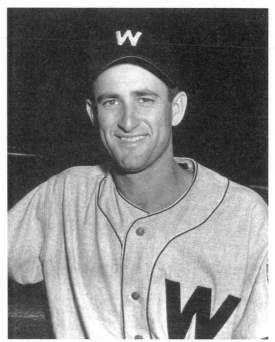

Traded away from the Senators in 1949, Vernon returned to the club in 1950.

his own good," the man known as The Old Fox said. "I hated to send him away. But that's baseball. I think it may be what he needs. A change of scenery sometimes does wonders for a ballplayer."

It certainly didn't bother Vernon. "I felt great," he said. "I knew I was going to a pretty good team with a chance to get to the World Series again. "I didn't mind leaving Washington."

With Cleveland, Vernon was joining a star-studded cast that included future Hall of Famers Lou Boudreau, the manager, Larry Doby, Bob Feller, Bob Lemon, Satchel Paige, and his old teammate Early Wynn, who would become his roommate. Also included in this august group were such stalwarts as Dale Mitchell, Joe Gordon, Ken Keltner, Jim Hegan, Mike Garcia, and Gene Beardon. All were among the higher echelon of the baseball kingdom. Washington was never like this.

Vernon was joining a star-studded infield that included Keltner at third, Boudreau at short, and Gordon at second. At one time or another, all were all-stars. "He certainly looks good," said Boudreau. "I think Mickey's going to help this infield a whole lot."

Mickey also expected that his new team would provide a big boost to his offense. "Playing with the Indians," he said, "should add 20 points to my batting average because I could never hit their pitchers, Feller, Lemon, and Beardon."

Joining the Indians would also allow Mickey to stage a reunion with his one-time Navy buddy, Doby; his former nemesis and barnstorming chief Feller; and later in the season, the young third baseman he had seen play in the Navy, Al Rosen.

From all indications, happy days were here again for Vernon. And he could hardly wait to get to spring training.

But first, Mickey had more pressing business. In February, he entered Chester Hospital and underwent an appendectomy. Ironically, Vernon's buddy Danny Murtaugh had undergone the same procedure just a few weeks earlier. Vernon spent eight days in the hospital before eventually heading with Lib by train to the Indians' camp at Tucson, Arizona.

Once there, though, Vernon eased into the starting lineup. Then, early in the season, he ventured into a new field. He had a part in a baseball movie called *The Kid from Cleveland*. A number of other Indians were in the film, including Hegan, Boudreau, Keltner, Paige, Feller, and utility infielder Johnny Berardino, who later enjoyed a real acting career, including playing the role of Dr. Steve Hardy in the long-running television soap, *General Hospital*.

"The movie was shot in the morning," Vernon recalled. "Boudreau had suggested that everybody get the same pay. When Feller heard that, he said, 'Anybody want to buy my share?' Our big scene was at a boys' detention home. I even had a line. A kid said to me, 'What do I have to do to be a good first baseman?' I said, 'Keep your eye on the ball and grow up tall.' "

Once the season began, Vernon immediately demonstrated the wisdom of the trade from a Cleveland standpoint. In the Indians' home opener—on Mickey's birthday—his 10th inning single off Dizzy Trout drove in Doby from second to give the Tribe a 4-3 victory over the Tigers. Later in the season, Trout would hit Vernon with a pitch, then invite him to fight by yelling, "Come on out." "If I do," Mickey shouted back, "I'll bring this bat with me." The bout didn't happen.

Shortly after his opening day heroics, Vernon's bases-loaded, 11th inning single chased home the winning run and combined with a four-hitter by Wynn to defeat the Chicago White Sox, 3-2. Then Vernon gave Feller and Cleveland a 4-2 decision over the Yankees with a two-run homer in the 11th. That was followed by a two-run double and a RBI single to produce a 4-2 verdict for Wynn over the Red Sox. A few days later, Mickey drilled a two-run triple in the eighth inning to hand the Chisox a 5-3 loss.

Vernon's offensive barrage led the Indians to victory in eight of their first nine games. And Mickey was flying high. "This looks like the opportunity of my baseball career," he said.

But the Cleveland Indians of 1949 were not the same team as the one the year before. Instead of waging a strong defense of their title, the team slipped to third place, eight games behind the front-running Yankees. In one of the greatest seasons of all time with all five members of the American League's ruling class finishing above .500, the Yankees edged the Red Sox by one game in a torrid two-team duel that went down to the last game of the season.

There was good news on the Vernon front, though. Mickey regained his batting touch, and finished with a .291 average, 49 points above his mark in 1948. His home run production also soared to 18 and he collected 83 RBI. On defense, Vernon had a spectacular season. He set American League records for first basemen for most putouts (1,438) and most assists (155) in one season.

That winter, Mickey took a job selling games in the toy department of Gimbels in downtown Philadelphia. And again the trade winds blew. The Chicago White Sox offered to swap pitcher Bill Wight for Vernon or second baseman Cass Michaels for Vernon and Berardino. Indians general manager Hank Greenberg turned down both proposals. He also vetoed offers for Vernon from the Yankees, Red Sox, and Tigers.

What the former home run king didn't turn down, though, was the chance to send Mickey to the bench. The reason: a hulking former Negro League first baseman named Luke Easter.

Easter, a 6-foot 4½-inch 240-pounder, had been touted as the new Josh Gibson when he joined the Homestead Grays in 1947. That never happened. After two years with the Pittsburgh-based

Grays, who ironically played many of their home games at Washington's Griffith Stadium, Easter was sold to Cleveland for $10,000 and was sent to the Pacific Coast League where he played with the San Diego Padres who—in another ironic twist—were managed by Bucky Harris.

After hitting .363 with 25 home runs and 83 RBI in a mere 80 games, Easter was summoned to Cleveland. The Indians had been the first American League team to sign an African-American player when they landed Doby in 1947, and with Paige and now Easter in the organization, the club was at the forefront of the move to integrate big league baseball.

Once in Cleveland, Easter appeared in 25 games, but hit just .222 with no home runs and two RBI. Nevertheless, the Indians, anxious to add a power-hitter to their lineup, regarded Easter as their first baseman of the future.

At spring training in 1950, Easter, regularly putting his long-distance clouting on display, was the talk of the camp. Greenberg had an idea. He approached Vernon and asked, "Did you ever play the outfield?"

"I said, 'No, except in American Legion ball,'" Vernon recalled. "He said, 'Would you like to try it?' I was trying to get a little extra money, so I said, sure, if he'd give me $5,000 more on my contract. He said, 'I can't do that.'

"I said, 'Well, I remember a first baseman who moved to left field where he'd never played before.' Of course, I was referring to Greenberg himself, who the Tigers moved to left when they got Rudy York to play first base. But he still wouldn't give me the money, so I never played out there."

But Vernon didn't play much at first, either. Easter was installed as the regular man at the initial sack, and Mickey was relegated mostly to the bench. The few times he did play, it was usually against a lefthanded pitcher. It was not a pleasant situation for Mickey, but he understood what was happening.

"Cleveland was enamored with Easter," he said. "He was hitting well. They had to play him. But there wasn't room for both

Mickey got to meet numerous movie stars, including
June Allyson in 1949.

of us. No way we could share duties. I knew something was
going to happen."

Unlike many other situations in which two players are battling
for the same job, there was no animosity between Vernon and
Easter. "He was a really nice guy," Mickey said. "In fact, later on,
whenever I came to Cleveland, he always offered to let me borrow
his car, although I never did."

At one point, the Indians tried to trade Mickey to—of all
places—New York. The Yankees were badly in need of a first
baseman because Tommy Henrich, their regular at that position,
was ailing and unable to play. The trade fell through, but that
didn't end Cleveland's attempts to strike a deal somewhere else.

"I was at a movie in Cleveland, and I found out Greenberg
was trying to find me," Vernon remembered. "He finally got hold
of me, and told me I'd been traded back to Washington. I didn't
say anything. I just packed up and went to St. Louis where the

Senators were playing. I was glad to be traded, but not back to Washington."

The June 14 trade was basically engineered by Boudreau with the blessing of club president Ellis Ryan, who had replaced the colorful pioneer, Bill Veeck. In exchange for Mickey, Cleveland got pitcher Dick Weik, a virtual unknown who would win only six games—one as an Indian—in his entire big league career. Ultimately, the trade and the Indians' fourth place finish in 1950 cost Boudreau his job.

In an article written a few years later, Frank Gibbons of the Cleveland *Press* called it "one of the worst deals ever made." Vernon, he wrote, "was still one of the league's most valuable first sackers and worth about $200,000 to any team that needed his talents. Weik was a promising pitcher, but worth little more than the waiver price. "

Nevertheless, Vernon was back with the Senators, like it or not. And the club had a new manager, a fellow by the name of Bucky Harris. For Harris, it was his third stint with the Senators during a managerial career that extended from 1928 to 1956 and would conclude with his election to the Hall of Fame.

The likeable Harris, always one of Vernon's staunchest supporters, was thrilled to be reunited with the slim slugger. "He's my kind of player," the skipper said. "I'd rather have him up there in the clutch than anybody I know."

Washington's roster had changed considerably since Vernon had left the club. Second baseman Michaels, outfielder Irv Noren, and pitchers Connie Marrero, Bob Kuzava, and Sandy Consuegra were now with the team.

It was somewhat ironic that Vernon rejoined the Senators in St. Louis. By then, Veeck, the classic showman, had left the Indians and had taken control of the lowly Browns. Veeck had always been a big Mickey Vernon fan, and after bringing him to Cleveland, had made numerous attempts to get him for his new club.

Burton Hawkins, writing in *Baseball Digest*, claimed that over the years Veeck had made at least "30 propositions" to get Vernon.

"He's a smart ballplayer—a good hitter, a good fielder, and a real nice fellow," Veeck said. When Greenberg swapped Vernon, he added, "Washington made one of the great deals of all time. They picked up a whale of a player for a pitcher who can't win."

Vernon liked Veeck, too. "I always thought he was good for baseball," Mickey said. "He usually filled the park, and he was the first one to bring African-American players into the American League. That took a lot of courage in those days. He was an interesting guy. One time he invited me to his house when he was living on the Eastern Shore, and he showed me his record collection. He had thousands of records. He was also a big reader of books. He was constantly reading a book."

Following the series in St. Louis, the Senators moved on to Cleveland. Having managed Easter the previous year, Harris had the strategy for pitching to him all mapped out.

"Don't throw him slow, off-speed stuff," Harris told his pitchers. "Crowd him with fastballs." The first time Easter came to bat, Joe Haynes was on the mound for Washington. The count went to 3-0. Then Haynes threw Easter a changeup. Luke hit it into the upper deck at cavernous Municipal Stadium.

So much for strategy. And by the end of the season, it was so much for any semblance of a winner in Washington. In an astonishing separation between the haves and the have nots, four American League teams—New York, Detroit, Boston, and Cleveland (in that order) all won more than 90 games. And the four other teams each lost more than 85 games with the Senators having the lowest loss total at 87, which got them a fifth-place finish.

Rejuvenated in Washington, Vernon hit .306 in 90 games with the Senators to wind up the season with an overall .281 average. Easter, by the way, would have three big seasons as a regular with Cleveland, but was gone from the majors in 1954.

While Vernon cavorted on the field with his usual style and grace, he also attracted the attention of youngsters watching him from the stands. One was Dick Heller. For him, it would be the start of a long and happy relationship with the angular first baseman.

Although he suffered few injuries in his career, Vernon pulled a muscle running to third base.

"I became a Senators fan in 1949 when I was 11 years old," said Heller, who later spent his working career as a sportswriter with papers such as the Washington *Evening Star*, the Arlington (Virginia) *Sun*, and the Washington *Times*. "I remember that there was such an uproar around town when Mickey was traded that Griffith had to bring him back.

"He was the most graceful first baseman I ever saw. He made everything look so effortless. I can't imagine him ever being awkward. He was very instinctive. He was a good hitter, too, but I remember him more as a fielder than as a hitter. After every putout at first base that ended the inning, he'd look intently at the ball before throwing it back to the mound. He wanted to make sure that the ball wasn't scuffed when the Senators came to bat. My impression of him was that he was a guy who loved the game, and got a lot of fun out of it."

Individually, the game might have been fun for Vernon. But it wasn't much fun playing in Washington, especially in 1951 when the Senators lost 92 games and finished in seventh place, 10 games ahead of the hapless Browns but 36 games behind the top-ranked Yankees.

As he usually did in Washington, Vernon had spent the off-season dickering with Griffith over salary. And there was constant speculation that he would be traded—back to the Indians, or to the Browns, to the Yankees, to Detroit—nearly everybody seemed to have an interest in Vernon.

Mickey finally signed for $21,000. The money came in handy. After living with Lib's parents for 11 years, the Vernons had moved to a new home in Wallingford. A handsome house in a lovely neighborhood, it would be home for the Vernons for the next 52 years.

In the first month of the 1951 season, Mickey had a hand in one of the most unusual games of the year. On April 26, Washington's Marrero pitched a one-hitter to beat the Athletics, 2-1. Gil Coan and Vernon homered for the Senators off Joe Coleman. The A's only hit came on a home run by Barney McCosky. Three runs, three homers.

Five days later, Mickey's 13th-inning home run off Cliff Fannin beat the Browns, 9-8. Then he smoked two two-run homers and a single off Vic Raschi to hand the Senators a 4-1 win over the Yankees.

With his bat continuing to regain its old magic, Vernon finished the season with a .293 average. He hit nine home runs and drove in 87. The Nats wound up in seventh place.

As was always the case during the off-season, Vernon could often be seen around Marcus Hook. He was even a judge at the boro's annual Halloween Day parade. "It was not unusual to see him just standing on the corner signing autographs," said Ernie Montella, who grew up in Hook near where Mickey lived. "All the kids looked up to him. He was our idol. He was a celebrity, but you'd never know it."

Despite his fine performance the previous year—which also included leading first baseman in fielding percentage for the sec-

They didn't often cross paths during the season, but Danny Murtaugh and Mickey hooked up before an exhibition game in 1951.

ond straight year—Vernon was not only not offered a pay raise in 1952, Griffith wanted to cut his salary by $4,000. Mickey's annual salary squabble resulted in his signing again for $21,000.

With Vernon now approaching the age of 34, there were whispers that he was slowing down a bit, despite his performance the previous year. Mickey took steps himself to prevent such an occurrence. He talked in spring training to Hall of Famer Tris Speaker, one of the greatest hitters of all time, about using a lighter bat. Vernon tried it, and it worked—with resounding results.

Early in the 1952 season, he hit a home run into the third tier at Yankee Stadium and also singled twice in three trips to the plate to give the Senators a 2-0 victory.

Three months later, a very special event took place in the Vernon family. On July 25, Lib gave birth to a girl. She was named Gay Anne. "She changed our lives quite a bit," Vernon said.

Later in the season, in an interview with Arthur Richman, Vernon noted: "Any success I enjoy has to be credited to my wife and our new baby girl. Lib is a wonderful, understanding person, and I guess I'd be lost without her. A ballplayer's wife has to put up with a lot of hardships and unpleasantness, but I never hear her complain. As for our little girl, she's the biggest thing in our lives. I don't want to sound like I'm popping off, but with Gay Anne offering me inspiration, I feel spry enough to stick around the majors for quite a number of years."

By the end of the season—one in which the Senators finished fifth—Vernon had slumped to one of the lowest levels of his career, hitting just .251. Although he had 10 home runs and 80 RBI, it was not what Dr. Speaker had ordered.

It would be a long winter back home for Mickey. But there was light at the end of the tunnel.

Another Batting Title

The kid could play. Mickey Vernon could tell that right away.

Vernon saw him playing a day in 1944 during one of the many service games military base teams in the same region played against each other during World War II. Mickey was playing for Norfolk Air Station. The kid wore the uniform of Camp Shelton, a Virginia Navy base.

He was only 19. Despite his youth, he had already played one year in the minor leagues as a member of the Cleveland Indians organization. He was playing for a base team that included several major league players. That was awesome enough, but it was nothing compared to what happened after the game with Norfolk.

As the teenager was walking off the field, Vernon approached him. Mickey was impressed with the way he handled the bat. Shaking hands and introducing himself, Vernon gave him some words of encouragement. "You're good," he told him. "You look like you're going to be a big league player someday."

Vernon, of course, was right. The kid did make the majors. His name was Al Rosen.

Rosen and Vernon would cross paths many more times over the ensuing years. When Mickey was traded to the Indians in 1949, the club was getting Rosen ready to take over third base. Although Rosen had appeared briefly in previous seasons, his first full year came in 1950 when he led the American League in home runs. Vernon was with the Indians that year until mid-June. Many years later—in 1978—when he was president and general manager of the New York Yankees, Rosen would hire Vernon as a roving minor league hitting instructor.

But it was in between those two connections that the two would become inexorably linked. The year was 1953. It was the year Rosen and Vernon fought for an American League batting title that was not decided until the final at-bat of the season.

By then, Rosen was firmly entrenched as one of the premier players in the league. After his 1950 season when he had hit .287 with 37 home runs and 116 RBI, he had become a two-time All-Star and had led the league with 105 RBI in 1952, a year in which he hit .302. The stocky third-sacker played a major role on an Indians team that won more than 90 games three straight years between 1950 and 1953 before capturing the AL pennant in 1954.

Meanwhile, Vernon was seven years removed from his first batting crown, and had, in fact, not hit .300 since then. Soon after the 1953 season began, Mickey would pass his 35th birthday. He had hit just .251 the year before, and the whispers were starting to mount that maybe the popular first baseman was nearing the end of the trail.

"A rank visionary who suggested that Mickey would win another batting crown," wrote columnist Shirley Povich in the Washington *Post*, "would have been hauled off to the lunatic ward."

The winter of 1952-53 had not been terribly enjoyable for Mickey. He underwent surgery twice, once for a tumor in his mouth, once for a fissure in his backside. Both ailments had given him ample doses of pain during the previous season, probably contributing to his depleted batting average.

Griffith Stadium was not an easy place for lefthanded batters to hit. Ones such as Vernon often sprayed hits to the spacious left side of the field.

During the off-season, Senators owner Clark Griffith shopped Vernon around the league. He told writers "there was a good chance for a deal." The most likely customer was again the Yankees, who had made another one of their frequent moves to get Mickey.

To get Vernon, Griffith wanted the Yankees to give up Jackie Jensen, a promising young outfielder, and Joe Collins, a veteran but unspectacular first baseman. When the Yankees rejected the proposal, Griffith completely reversed his position. "Why should we trade Vernon?" he said. "Nobody gives you a better job at first base."

Although Jensen would be swapped to the Senators in a multi-player deal in May, Vernon stayed put. But once again, the miserly Griffith cut his salary. Mickey signed for $18,500.

Unlike most of his other years in Washington, though, Vernon was playing with a fairly decent team. The 1952 Senators had finished two games over .500. The '53 team, which would wind up at an even .500, had a strong infield that included Vernon, Wayne

Terwilliger at second base, Pete Runnels at shortstop, and Eddie Yost at third, and Jensen, Jim Busby, and Clyde Vollmer in the outfield. Ed Fitzgerald caught a respectable pitching staff that included eventual 22-game winner Bob Porterfield, Frank Shea, Walt Masterson, and Chuck Stobbs.

The 1953 season began handsomely for Vernon, who Philadelphia *Evening Bulletin* Hall of Fame baseball writer Ray Kelly once described as being "lean, lanky and likeable." Mickey went two-for-three with a double in the Senators' opener on April 16, then duplicated that feat in the third game. But after going hitless in five of the first 14 games, Vernon finished the month hitting just .255.

Rosen, meanwhile, hit safely in each of the Indians' 11 April games and ended the month carrying a .361 average.

At the beginning of May, Vernon's two-run homer carried the Senators to a 5-4 victory over the St. Louis Browns. Then on May 3, Vernon launched a 20-game hitting streak that didn't end until May 28 when he was stopped by the Yankees and Whitey Ford. The streak was bolstered by a four-hit game in an 8-3 Washington victory on May 20 over Cleveland and Bob Feller, two three-hit games, and nine games in which he laced two hits. The surge vaulted Mickey into the lead with a .366 average. Going 4-for-23 after the streak ended, Vernon finished May with a .339 mark, trailing Rosen, who had four three-hit games during the month, by one point.

Feller, as always, was suitably impressed. "Mickey was always hard to pitch to," he recalled many years later. "He hit high and he hit low pitches. He didn't really have a weakness. He hit the ball wherever it was pitched. The only thing I could do was move the ball around and mix up my pitches."

Other pitchers were having trouble with Vernon, too. Bobby Shantz of the Philadelphia Athletics had been the American League's Most Valuable Player the year before after posting a sparkling 24-7 record. But even though he was lefthanded, Shantz was never thrilled about the prospects of facing Vernon.

"I had a hard time getting him out," Shantz recalled. "I tried to get him out with curveballs. I didn't want to throw him fastballs because he was a good fastball hitter. And he hit those line drives all the time. But he could hit the ball out of the park, too. He stood pretty far away from the plate, but his bat covered the plate real well. He was just so damn tough to pitch to."

The battle between Vernon and Rosen raged on into June. But by then, another hitter had entered the race. New York's Mickey Mantle threw his hat into the ring with a red-hot May.

On June 7, Vernon's three hits and four RBI led a 16-2 assault of the Chicago White Sox. One week later, he clubbed a two-run home run in a 6-1 victory over the Detroit Tigers. Three days after that, his bases-loaded single with two outs in the ninth inning gave the Senators a 1-0 victory over the White Sox. At that point, Mickey held a three-point lead over Mantle, .335 to .332. Vernon retained the lead as June ended with a .327 average. Rosen, meanwhile, dropped back to .317.

In July, a slump by Mantle knocked him well off the pace. For Vernon, though, it was a big month.

"I think he's better now than he ever was," said Washington manager Bucky Harris. "He's a great team man, too. He fools you because he's so lackadaisical, but that's just his way. He's got plenty of hustle and fight. You can take all the dangerous hitters in the American League, but the guy I'd like to see up there for me in the clutch is Vernon."

Mickey began a hitting streak on July 11, and it went on for 18 straight games until Chicago's Virgil Trucks finally brought it to a halt on July 30. Included in the spree were a three-RBI game in a 6-4 win over Cleveland, and two singles and a three-run homer in a 13-5 triumph over the Tigers. The streak meant that Vernon had hit in 25 of his last 26 games with his average during that time jumping from .323 to .332.

The All-Star Game was scheduled to be held July 14 at Cincinnati's Crosley Field, and as the game approached, Mickey was reeling in the votes from far and wide. By the time the final count was tallied, Vernon was the third highest vote-getter, rank-ing behind only Mantle and Yogi Berra and ahead of players such as Phil Rizzuto, Nellie Fox, Stan Musial, Ralph Kiner, Roy Campanella, and Eddie Mathews, all future Hall of Famers. Mickey polled 1,112,763 votes, which far outdistanced the other leading American League first basemen, including defending bat-ting champ Ferris Fain, Eddie Robinson, Walt Dropo, and Collins.

After the votes were counted, Mickey went to the office of the Washington *Times-Herald* and typed a letter to fans, thanking them for their votes. "The privilege of playing in the 1953 All-Star con-test," he wrote, "is another pleasant memory that I can take with me when I lay aside the old bat and glove."

In what would be his third All-Star Game and second as a starter, Vernon went hitless in three trips to the plate. He flew out in the first inning against Robin Roberts of the Philadelphia Phillies and struck out twice against the Milwaukee Braves' Warren Spahn as the National League captured a 5-1 victory.

But Vernon's bat remained the focal point of everyone's atten-tion, and it wasn't slowing down. The big games continued. On August 18, Mickey's home run and three-run triple featured a seven-run ninth-inning rally in which the Senators downed the Yankees, 10-8, at Yankee Stadium. Three three-hit games helped Vernon end the month with a .329 average. Rosen, having gone on a 10-game hitting streak in mid-August, finished the month at .325.

Asked by writers how he accounted for his glowing success, Vernon gave a plausible explanation. "I'm meeting the ball better than I have in a long time," he said. "Maybe my coordination is getting better. The ball seems to be going off my bat a lot faster. I'm not trying to overpower anybody. I'm not strong enough to do that. I simply try to hit the ball where it's pitched; outside ones to left, inside ones to right. I guess I'm getting my 184 pounds into every swing."

Vernon continued his heavy hitting in September—with a lit-tle help from his friends. In the third inning of a game early in the month against the Yankees, Mickey hit a grounder to Rizzuto. The shortstop bobbled the ball and was given an error by official scorer Bob Addie of the Washington *Post*. A little while later, Rizzuto called Addie in the press box and told him that the ball had hit a pebble and that he thought Vernon would've beaten the throw anyway. After the game—a 22-1 romp by New York—Addie conferred with umpire Art Passarella, who agreed with Rizzuto. Addie reversed his call and gave Vernon a hit.

On September 9, in the midst of a 14-game hitting streak, Mickey belted a game-tying single in the 10th inning and a game-winning double in the 12th to give Washington a 2-1 victory over the Browns in the second game of a doubleheader. Four days later, he went 5-for-7 with four singles, a home run, two walks, and a hit-by-pitch in 10-4 and 6-4 doubleheader losses to the Tigers (a team against which Vernon would compile a .494 batting average that season). The splurge hiked Vernon's batting average to .337, good for an eight-point lead over Rosen.

But Al wasn't letting up. During an 11-game hitting streak, he had a three-hit game on September 7, another three-hit game on September 12, and by the middle of the month, his average was .330. Vernon was hitting .339.

Throughout the season, the two contenders had continued their friendship from earlier years. Once, during the campaign, Rosen even interviewed Vernon on a radio show. "You'd have thought we were going to meet in the ring, there was so much ado over the race," Mickey said. "The Cleveland and Washington papers were filled with stories all season."

When their teams met and Rosen would get to first, he and Vernon would chat about their families; never about the batting race. "We had been good friends since we were in Cleveland together," Rosen remembered. "Mickey and Lib were always awfully nice to me. Of course, Mickey was a wonderful guy, very gentle, very quiet, elegant. He was very reserved, just the opposite of me."

All the while, Rosen, whose nickname was Flip, had two other batting matters weighing heavily on his hands. He was fighting the Athletics' Gus Zernial for the home run title and was running away with the RBI crown. A batting championship, too, would give him only the seventh Triple Crown in American League history and the first since Ted Williams performed the feat in 1947.

A considerable amount of attention was focused on Rosen. The pressure was much heavier on him than it was on Vernon. But then again, Mickey never felt much pressure when he was playing anyway.

"There wasn't any pressure on me," he said. "I just took each game one at a time. I was just trying to do my best. I never worried if I didn't get a hit in a game. And if I got two hits, I wanted to get three. If I got three, I wanted to get four. I always wanted more. But that wasn't what I would call pressure."

On September 20, Vernon got a much-needed respite from the hectic race when Delaware County fans honored him between games of a doubleheader at the newly named Connie Mack Stadium. The day was declared Mickey Vernon Day in Delaware County. It took 16 buses and 150 cars to get some 1,500 fans, including 400 Little Leaguers dressed in their uniforms, to the event.

For many months, Vernon's friends, led by chairman Al Duffy, the postmaster in Elwyn, had been going door to door, holding covered dish dinners, benefit softball games, tag days, and doing whatever else it took to raise funds for gifts that would be presented to Mickey. Enough money was raised to purchase a variety of gifts, the biggest of which was a new Pontiac Catalina with a chartreuse roof.

The car was driven around the field by Mickey's friend Harvey Wood of Eddystone, afterwhich it was presented to the stunned player, along with many other gifts. Even Vernon's teammates chipped in, giving him a set of golf clubs that were presented by Yost.

Mickey, who had a double and two singles in five trips to the plate in the first game, went 0-for-5 in the nightcap. The Senators lost, 13-9 and 4-3. During the second game, the Athletics' Eddie

Mickey and Lib celebrated a new car and other gifts
presented by Delaware County fans on Mickey
Vernon day in 1953 at Connie Mack Stadium.

Robinson, after reaching first, said he'd give Mickey $2,150 for the
car. Vernon declined, saying he had better offers.

Back to reality, the batting race boiled down to the last weekend of the season. Mickey totted a .336 average, while Rosen followed at .329. Each batter had gone without a hit in just two games
during the month.

On Friday, September 25, with the Senators playing host to the
Athletics at Griffith Stadium, Vernon failed to get a hit in four at-
bats. At the same time, with the Indians meeting the Tigers, Rosen
went 4-for-6, with two home runs and four RBI. Mickey's lead
dropped to one point.

The next day, Vernon stroked three singles in four at-bats,
while Rosen managed a pair of singles in four trips to the plate.
Mickey's average rose to .336, three points higher than Rosen's.

The Indians, hoping to improve the power-hitting Rosen's chances for the batting and home run titles, installed him in the leadoff spot throughout the weekend. And in Cleveland as well as in Washington, hardly a soul was not riveted to the race as it went down to the final day of the season.

At Cleveland's Municipal Stadium, the public address announcer gave an account of what happened in not only each at-bat for Vernon, but each at-bat for Zernial. In the press box, writers heard a play-by-play account of the game. Writers also listened to the game in the press box at Griffith Stadium where a tiny crowd of 3,740 showed up to see if Vernon could withstand Rosen's challenge.

In his first four trips to the plate, Rosen smacked a double and two singles off Tigers pitcher Al Aber. Meanwhile, Vernon beat out a bunt and singled cleanly to right in four trips to the plate against A's hurler Joe Coleman. In his last at-bat, Vernon lined a foul ball over the fence in right, just missing a home run. On the next pitch, Mickey laced a hard liner to right that was caught by Elmer Valo, whose catches had helped Vernon win the batting title in 1946.

Rosen came to bat for the final time in the bottom of the ninth. Knowing he needed a hit to pass Vernon, he went to a 3-2 count on Aber, then fouled off several pitches that were out of the strike zone. Finally, he slapped a high chopper to Gerry Priddy at third. Rosen knew it would be a close play, and as Priddy's throw reached first base, Al leaped toward the bag in a desperate attempt to beat the throw. But he landed four or five inches short of the base. Umpire Hank Soar called him out.

Indians manager Al Lopez raced from the dugout to argue that his man was safe. "I told him," Rosen recalled, "'Al, I was out. The umpire was right.' I told Soar, too, that he'd made the right call. He knew I was out. I knew I was out. Fred Hutchinson [Detroit's manager] knew I was out. He said he wouldn't have argued if I'd been called safe. Priddy said he thought I was safe.

"Had Soar made a sympathy call and ruled me safe," Rosen

In a highly unusual play for a first baseman, Vernon has just tagged out Minnie Minoso of the Chicago White Sox at home plate.

said, "I would have felt less of myself. Asked at the time why he didn't bunt with Priddy playing back, Rosen had a similar thought. "I didn't want to win it that way," he said.

The race, however, was not over. Because Cleveland's 9-3 loss ended before Washington's eventual 9-2 defeat, folks at Griffith Stadium knew that Rosen had made an out in his last at-bat, and thus ended with three-for-five for the day. As the Senators came to bat in the bottom of the eighth, Harris called the press box. He was told that Vernon had a lead of .0011 and even if he went out in his last trip to the plate, he had the title sewed up. Harris, however, refused to believe what he was being told.

Harris wanted to take Vernon out so he wouldn't have to bat again, but decided against it because "Mickey wouldn't have stood for it," he said. Vernon's teammates didn't want to take any chances, and they had another idea of how to handle the situation. They would make sure Mickey wouldn't come to bat again.

In the bottom of the eighth, Busby and Jerry Snyder made easy outs. But a grounder by Mickey Grasso took an unexpected bounce into the third base bag. As the ball caromed away, Grasso had no choice but to jog to second with a double. The resourceful Grasso then took matters into his own hands by getting picked off second.

That left one more inning for the Senators. And as they came to bat in the bottom of the ninth, Vernon was scheduled to be the fourth hitter. Leading off the inning, pinch-hitter Kite Thomas, batting for Masterson, singled, but tried leisurely to stretch the hit into a double and was thrown out at second. The next batter was Yost, owner of one of the best eyes in the game. He swung at a pitch over his head and popped out. That left matters up to Runnels, a future two-time batting champ. With Vernon crouched in the on-deck circle, Pete taped a half-hearted grounder to second, ran down the line slowly, and was thrown out by a large margin. The game was over. Vernon had won the batting crown.

As the game came to an end, an announcement that Vernon had won the title was greeted by a thunderous cheer from the miniature crowd. In the clubhouse, Mickey's teammates swarmed all over him in a joyous celebration.

Asked by reporters to cite the reasons for his success, Vernon had a typically modest answer. "It's a simple formula," he said. "When the ball falls in right, you get a hit. When it doesn't, you don't."

Mickey finished with a .337 batting average. At 35, he was at the time the oldest player to win an AL batting crown. He was also the first Washington player to win two batting titles. Vernon also led the AL in doubles with 43, while collecting a team-leading 15 home runs. Vernon had a career high 115 RBI, which ranked second in the league and which made him the first Senator to drive in 100 or more runs since Stan Spence did it in 1944. He also placed second in the league in hits with 205 and in total bases with 315, and fifth in slugging average (.518).

Vernon's batting title was part of what was a remarkable year for baseball-playing Pennsylvanians. Philadelphian Roy Campanella won the National League's Most Valuable Player Award, and Carl Furillo of Reading was the NL batting champion. Both played with the Brooklyn Dodgers.

Denied of the Triple Crown, Rosen wound up with a .336 batting average. While losing the batting crown by one point, he beat Zernial by one home run to win the title with 43. Rosen also led the league in RBI (145), runs (115), total bases (367), and slugging average (.613). He was chosen the AL's Most Valuable Player and was named Player of the Year by *The Sporting News.*

After Rosen in the batting race, no one else was close. The Red Sox's Billy Goodman and the White

The race went down to the final at-bat of the season before Mickey won his second batting title.

Sox's Minnie Minoso each hit .313. Busby followed at .312. Mantle was far down the list with a .295 mark.

One-half century later, Rosen was still gracefully accepting his loss in the torrid batting race that he had waged with his friend. "Mickey won it. I lost it," he said. "That was the end of it. I have no remorse. Of course, I would've liked to have won the title, but Mickey just had a better year than I did. Mickey was a professional. He was a very competent hitter, and anybody who played the game as well as he did deserved to win the title. It may sound trite, but I was really more disappointed that we didn't win the pennant."

For the top two hitters, it had been one of the tightest batting races in major league history. But for Vernon, his baseball activities for the year were not over. After the season, he was one of 32 players who joined Hall of Famer Jimmie Foxx on a nationwide tour to fight juvenile delinquency. Players traveled in groups of four with all 48 states visited by at least one group.

When the tour ended, Vernon came home to Wallingford. And a much-needed rest.

Ike's Favorite Player

One of the more unencumbered duties of the President of the United States while the Washington Senators existed was to throw out the first ball on opening day each year. Symbolically, the Washington opener, held one day before all other openers, launched the major league baseball season.

Throwing out the first ball in Washington was a practice that dated back to 1912 when the portly righthander William Howard Taft made the first presidential pitch. In the years that followed, 10 more commanders in chief performed the annual rite for either the original or expansion versions of the Senators.

For most of the presidents, the first game of the baseball season was a pleasant diversion from the more serious duties of the office. It gave them a chance to mix with the baseball crowd instead of with heads of state, other politicians, and bureaucrats. At least from a political standpoint, the public attention that the event received wasn't without benefit, either.

The event also had a certain appeal to the players. Each year, members of both teams positioned themselves on the field near the president's box with the hope of catching the chief executive's toss. When he threw the ball, a mad scramble would result. The player who came up with the ball would be taken to the president, who would autograph it and give it back to him. Vernon seldom participated in the contest. "I would stand behind everybody and take pictures," he said. "I always enjoyed photography."

Of all the presidents who participated in the traditional opening day toss, none had a bigger interest in sports than the nation's 34th president, Dwight D. Eisenhower. Although a football star in his younger days, the former general liked many sports, not the least of which was baseball, which he had also played and which he followed avidly.

So it was that in the second year of his presidency, the man known far and wide simply as "Ike" met his favorite baseball player, Washington Senators first baseman Mickey Vernon.

In the months leading up to that game, it had been a busy winter for Vernon.

Mickey was often seen driving around his native Delaware County in the Pontiac that local fans had given him the previous year. The car bore a license tag with the number 337, his batting average the previous season. At the 50th anniversary banquet of the Philadelphia Sports Writers' Association, Vernon was cited for his batting title. Among others at the head table for this special evening were people with names such as Ty Cobb, Chuck Klein, Lefty Grove, Jimmie Foxx, Mickey Cochrane, Tris Speaker, Joe Louis, Red Grange, Jack Kelly Sr., and Willie Hoppe.

Vernon was once again embroiled in a contract battle with Senators' owner Clark Griffith. The miserly former big league pitcher had offered Vernon a new contract calling for a salary of $21,000. That represented a mere $2,500 raise for the defending American League batting champion and was actually the same salary as he had been paid in 1951.

"That's ridiculous," Vernon was quoted as saying. Mickey wanted $35,000, and said he would not go to spring training until he got it.

Among the honored guests at the 1954 Philadelphia Sports
Writers' Association banquet were batting rivals Mickey Vernon
and Al Rosen who discussed their race with Hall of Famer Ty Cobb

Griffith upped the offer to $22,000. When Vernon didn't
budge, the Nats' president made what he said would be his final
offer, $25,000. "Vernon," he said, "is the most difficult man I ever
dealt with on the salary question."   Griffith threatened to trade
Mickey to the Boston Red Sox, a team with an open spot at first
base that it wanted Vernon to fill. "I won't sell him, but I might
trade him if they offered me the right players," Griffith said.

No trade was made. And the salary impasse was finally broken in early March when Vernon signed for $30,000. That made
Mickey the second-highest-paid player in Senators history. He
trailed only Speaker, a future Hall of Famer, who earned a reported $55,000 in 1927 in his only season in Washington, his next to last
year as a player.

Having thus become owner of one of the American League's
highest salaries, Vernon joined his teammates for the rest of spring
training. Then opening day arrived in Washington on April 13.
Because the home opener had been rained out in 1953, and
Eisenhower was unable to attend the rescheduled event, this was
the first time the former general would throw out a first ball.

An overflow crowd of 27,160 was on hand as the Senators met
the New York Yankees, World Series winners in each of the previ-

ous five seasons. As was always the case on opening day, the stands were packed with Washington dignitaries.

The Yankees had tied the game in the top of the ninth inning, and the score was still 3-3 as the Senators came to bat in the bottom of the 10th. New York had summoned Allie Reynolds to the mound in relief. A fireballing righthander, Reynolds, who in 1951 had pitched two no-hitters, was one of the toughest hurlers in the league. He had won in double figures 12 years in a row while pitching for the Cleveland Indians and Yankees. Although a starter, Reynolds was occasionally asked to pitch in relief. This was one of those times.

It was getting dark and a little difficult to see as Reynolds began the inning by walking Eddie Yost. Nothing much to be embarrassed about that. Known as "The Walking Man," Yost usually drew more than 100 bases on balls each season, and during his 18-year career he led the league in that category six times.

The next batter was Tom Wright, and Reynolds struck him out with ease. Vernon, who was hitless in four trips to the plate and who had made an error, was next. As Mickey settled into the batter's box, he was not thinking about the right field wall that loomed just 328 feet down the line at Griffith Stadium. The wall, after all, was not something that lefthanded batters looked upon with any kind of fondness, its 31-foot-high surface stopping countless balls that would have otherwise gone for home runs.

Reynolds grooved a fastball. And like the versatile hitter he was, Vernon got around on it. The ball not only cleared the wall in right-center field, it ticked off a beer sign anchored above the scoreboard, giving the Senators a 5-3 victory. It was one of the longest balls Mickey ever hit at Griffith Stadium.

Yost, scoring ahead of Vernon, waited at home plate to greet the game-winning slugger. He was immediately joined by the rest of the Washington team, plus one other person.

"I felt this guy tugging on my sleeve," Vernon recalled. "He was wearing a suit and tie and a porkpie hat. I thought he was just some fan who'd jumped out of the stands."

President Dwight D. Eisenhower congratulates Vernon on his game-winning, opening-day home run.

"I'm a Secret Service agent," the guy said. "Come with me. The president wants to meet you."

Dutifully, Vernon hurried to the box beside the Senators' dugout where Eisenhower, having been been so excited that he'd tried to run out on the field before being discouraged by the Secret Service, was standing with his wife Mamie, along with Griffith and various cabinet members and other politicians. Griffith later told reporters that just before Vernon came to bat, Mrs. Eisenhower had pulled a rabbit's foot from her purse and told him to rub it for good luck.

At the box, an ecstatic president, who later revealed that Mickey was his favorite player, vigorously shook Vernon's hand. "Nice going. Wonderful, a wonderful home run," he said to Mickey. "We talked a little and he said he was glad to see me come through," Vernon recalled.

In the Yankees' clubhouse, Reynolds gave his version of the home run. "I was trying to get ahead of him in the count," he said, "and was trying to get a strike over the outside. The ball was a little bit outside, and I was liking it until I saw Mickey get his fat end of the bat on it. Only a real good hitter can step into an outside pitch and pull it like he did.

Eisenhower presented a silver bat to Mickey for his winning the batting title the previous season.

"Sometimes, things like that happen," Reynolds added. "It helped make the president's day a nice one, and it got the Washington club off to a nice start. Somehow, I'm not very sad about it. But I don't want these things to happen too often at my expense. I'm not that generous."

The home run was a sign of things to come. Not only did 20 of his first 33 hits go for extra bases, Vernon smacked nine four-baggers in his first 40 games, the last two coming during two games against the Philadelphia Athletics at Connie Mack Stadium. Mickey was in second place behind old friend Al Rosen in the home run race. The outburst of long-distance clouting was unusual for Vernon, and it didn't go unnoticed.

"Mickey Vernon is giving the Senators, as usual, a first base job that is the best in the league," wrote Shirley Povich in the Washington *Post*. More importantly, "Vernon at 36, has bloomed as a power-hitter at an age when most ballplayers have retired to slippers and the hearthstone. He shows little sign of acting his ripe baseball age, and is still the coltish fellow around the bag and on the bases."

As it turned out, Vernon's meeting on opening day with Eisenhower had a sequel. On May 27, the two crossed paths again.

This time the president came to Griffith Stadium to present his favorite player with a silver bat. At the time, bat manufacturer Hillerich & Bradsby awarded a silver bat each year to the winners of the American and National League batting titles. Considered one of the most prestigious honors in that era, the bat was valued at $500, but today is worth many times that amount.

No U.S. president had ever presented a silver bat before. Ike did it in a ceremony preceding once again a Senators game with the Yankees. The pre-game activities also included a performance by the U.S. Army Band. Players from both teams participated in a variety of contests, including egg-throwing, a blindfolded wheelbarrow race, long-distance fungo hitting, and accuracy throwing. Among others, Ethiopian emperor Haile Selassie was in the stands. Vernon's parents Pinker and Kate were also among the 23,483 in attendance.

When Eisenhower presented the bat to Vernon, he said: "Win it again, and I'll give you a gold one." And what was Mickey's response? "I don't quite remember," he said. "I was a bit flustered."

Vernon's anxiety over his second meeting in less than two months with the president may have spilled over into the game. He went hitless. The Senators, however, rallied with five unearned runs to beat New York, 7-3.

Mickey had one other noteworthy encounter with Eisenhower during Ike's presidency. As the story goes, according to Burton Hawkins writing in *Baseball Digest*, the old general was in his box at Griffith Stadium, and during the game Vernon drifted over near it for a pop foul. "Mr. President, you're looking a bit peaked," Vernon, the one-time pre-med student, said as he made the catch. "Try eating dandelions." Supposedly, Ike followed the advice, and the condition that bothered him immediately improved.

Meeting presidents, of course, was always one of the perks of playing with the Washington Senators. For the most part, the teams were never that good. Players had to be satisfied with hob-nobbing with the politicians.

"Eisenhower came out to the park quite a bit," Vernon remembered. "He would always wave and say hello. [Richard] Nixon and [John F.] Kennedy were big fans, too. Probably the biggest fan was Happy Chandler, who was a senator before he became the baseball commissioner. He, as did Nixon when he was vice president, often came into the clubhouse."

Surprisingly, Vernon never visited the White House. In 14 season openers during Mickey's various seasons in Washington, four different presidents—Franklin D. Roosevelt, Harry Truman, Eisenhower, and Kennedy—threw out opening day balls. "Ike had the strongest arm," Mickey said. "JFK had the best form. Truman could throw with either hand."

Vernon also encountered another person with political connections. Jacqueline Bouvier was a photographer with the Washington *Times-Herald* before she married JFK. Her work appeared in a weekly section called "The Inquiring Photographer." She visited Griffith Stadium on assignment one day and met Mickey, who it turned out was her favorite player, too.

At this point in his career, Vernon was at the top of the heap. When he visited New York, he dined at some of the top spots in the city, including Toots Shore's, where he met a young basketball coach, Senators fan, and fellow Washington resident named Red Auerbach. He went to the club of jazz great Eddie Condon one night with the Yankees' Tommy Henrich and pro football star Frank Gifford of the New York Giants, and far into the night after the joint had closed, the band was still going strong with Henrich at the piano. A friend of bandleader Harry James, Vernon once was seated at a table at a show with James' mother and his wife, actress Betty Grable. Vernon and the beauty queen even shared a dance that night. Another time, he and other Senators saw a Broadway performance of *Damn Yankees*, and Mickey was invited backstage to meet the star of the show, Gwen Verdon. And sometimes when he came to Philadelphia to perform, bandleader Tommy Dorsey stayed at the Vernons' house in Wallingford.

When Vernon received the silver bat from Eisenhower, he was just emerging from a deep slump. His average had dropped to

.147 at one point before it started to swing upward. "I thought I would hit the ball just as well as I did in '53," Vernon said. "But some of the balls that had fallen for hits the year before were being caught. They also started to play me a little better."

On May 23, however, Vernon's tie-breaking home run and three doubles paced a 15-hit Senators attack that clubbed the Philadelphia Athletics, 9-4. By the beginning of June, Vernon's average was up to .290, and he was among the league-leaders in home runs, triples, and doubles. In one game against the Athletics, he hit a home run and three doubles in four at-bats, giving him 11 hits in his last 21 at-bats. In another game, he went 5-for-7 against the Baltimore Orioles. And his average went over .300 for the first time all season.

"The swing is feeling good, and the bat is coming around nicely," Vernon told Povich.

On September 1, Vernon had another special day. In the first inning of an eventual 16-6 Senators win over the Detroit Tigers at Griffith Stadium, Mickey slashed a single off Ned Garver for the 2,000th hit of his career. In a prearranged plan with the umpires, the game was stopped as Washington third base coach George Myatt retrieved the ball and tossed it across the diamond to first base coach Heinie Manush, who stuck it in his pocket so he could give it to Vernon when the inning was over.

The hit vaulted Vernon into a highly select group. Just eight other players who'd worn the uniform of the Washington Senators had registered 2,000 hits. They were: Ed Delahanty, Sam Rice, Goose Goslin, Clyde Milan, Joe Judge, Manush, Joe Cronin, and Joe Kuhel. With the hit, Vernon joined Stan Musial and Enos Slaughter as the only active players with 2,000 or more hits. At the time, Vernon was just the 95th player in major league history to reach 2,000 hits.

"I wish I could get 2,000 more under you as manager," Vernon said to Senators' pilot Bucky Harris.

During the Senators' 18-hit barrage, Vernon picked up another single and his 19th home run of the season, which gave him the most homers for a lefthanded batter in Senators history. Earlier in the season, Vernon also collected his 1,000th career RBI and his 100th career triple.

Mickey stayed hot the rest of the season. Against the Red Sox, he singled, raced to third on Jim Busby's hit, and scored on a sacrifice fly by Chuck Stobbs to give the Senators an 8-7 victory in 15 innings. In an 8-1 triumph over the A's, he stroked a single, triple, and home run, and collected five RBI.

On September 22, Vernon had another kind of experience with the bat. He hit into

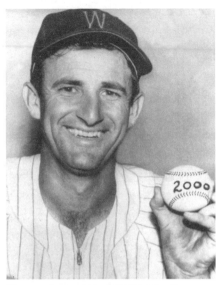

Vernon slugged his 2,000th hit off Ned Garver in a game late in the 1954 season.

a triple play. In a game against the Yankees, Vernon drilled a line drive that Bill Skowron caught at first base. Skowron stepped on the bag to retire Pete Runnels, then threw to Jerry Coleman at second to catch Wayne Terwilliger.

Vernon finished the season with a .290 batting average. He led the league in doubles with 33, was second to Minnie Minoso in total bases with 294, and placed third in triples (14) and fifth in slugging percentage (.492). He also led AL first basemen in fielding average (.992) and putouts (1365).

Other than the years in which he won batting titles, the 1954 season turned out to be one of the most memorable in Vernon's long career.

CHAPTER 13

Age Is No Barrier

W hat is the optimal age for a baseball player?

That is a question that even in this enlightened age of science and technology has no conclusive answer. It could be 28. It could be 30. It could be 32. Whatever the case, it's certainly not 35 or 36. Those are the years that a player is charitably said to be in "the twilight of his career."

By then, the back is aching. The legs feel like lead. The knees hurt. The shoulders throb. The arm is sore. The eyesight is not what it used to be. The reflexes have diminished. The concentration has become increasingly difficult to maintain. And the fire in the belly has been reduced to an occasional spark.

It is the unusual ballplayer who can overcome all of these obstacles and still perform at the levels of much younger men. Mickey Vernon was one of those unusual ballplayers.

In his mid-30s, when most players are contemplating the size of their retirement checks,

Vernon was having some of the best years of his career. For a guy who just a few years earlier was being told to dust off his rock-

Fans in Marcus Hook threw a parade for Mickey, who rode down the main street with Lib and Gay.

ing chair, it was a convincing case for the old Yogi Berra adage, "It's never over till it's over."

At age 35 in 1953, Vernon, who had fan clubs scattered around the Washington area, had become the oldest player ever to win an American League batting title. He followed that with a .290 season, then over the next two years staged the best back-to-back years in his career, hitting .301 in 1955 and .310 in 1956. At that point, Mickey was dottering along at the ripe old age of 38.

Much of Mickey's latent success was due to his penchant for clean living. As an editorial in the Chester *Times* put it, "Mickey Vernon lives the kind of life on and off the ball diamond that is worthy of emulation by all the baseball young fry in the country."

Despite his success, Vernon had struggled for recognition. "My dad always thought Mickey was undervalued by the fans, the writers, other players, and most of all Clark Griffith, who was cheap," said television host Maury Povich. "But he was a terrific player who played on some very bad teams."

Washington *Post* columnist Bob Addie underscored the absence of acclaim directed toward Vernon. "Of all the players

Although he was always considered an excellent base-runner, Vernon was tagged out at second on this play by the White Sox's Nellie Fox.

who ever made the Big Top," he wrote, "James Barton Vernon undoubtedly stands out as the most camouflaged (meaning obscured by Williams, DiMaggio, etc.). Vernon is so underrated by most fans (but not by players and managers) that he's almost obscure."

Once, while driving through Marcus Hook, New York *Herald-Tribune* columnist Red Smith asked his passenger, "What left-handed first baseman now active who won the batting championship of the American League in the last five years was born in this town?" The man guessed Ferris Fain, then Billy Goodman, Johnny Mize, Walt Dropo, Luke Easter, and Eddie Robinson. The name Mickey Vernon never occurred to him.

At least, Vernon was not undervalued in his native Marcus Hook. "Among the workers with the hard hats at Sun Oil or the customers at Imburgia's Café," wrote Al Cartwright in the Wilmington *News-Journal*, "you could talk baseball clear into the night shift and come away convinced that there is but a single player in all of the American League."

In typical Griffith style, the Senators' owner had cut Vernon's salary from $30,000 to $27,500 in 1955. Mickey got even less encouragement from his manager.

Chuck Dressen, who had spent time as skipper of the Cincinnati Reds and Brooklyn Dodgers—even winning two National League pennants with the Bums—had replaced Bucky Harris after the 1954 season. Dressen said that he would use Vernon only as a spot starter and pinch-hitter. "I probably won't play him in more than 100 games because of his age," Dressen said.

Little did Dressen realize at the time how wrong his assumption would be. Not only did Vernon play in 150 games for a Senators team that lost 101 outings and finished in last place 43 games below the top, he hit a sparkling .301 with 14 home runs and 85 RBI. Not bad for a 37-year-old has-been.

Along the way, Vernon was selected as the starting first baseman for the American League All-Star team. He played the entire game, getting one hit in five at-bats in a 12-inning, 6-5 triumph for the National League.

During the season, Mickey, never one to be the least bit affected by the color of a person's skin, also befriended a young, black Cuban player who had come up through the Senators' farm system and briefly joined the big club. Even though he played the same position as Vernon, Julio Becquer never forgot Mickey's kindness.

"I love the guy," said Becquer, who later spent four years with the Senators. "He is one of the great gentlemen in baseball. I admired him not only as a baseball player, but as a person. He always treated me very, very well."

By his own admission, when Becquer arrived in Washington late in the 1955 campaign, he was timid, scared, and uncertain. "I hardly knew any English, and it was very hard for me to communicate," he said. "But Mickey helped me so much. He made it easy for guys like me.

"I asked him about a lot of things," Becquer added. "I had a lot of questions about hitting. He had such a beautiful stroke. He always answered my questions. He also helped me with my fielding. He was just a beautiful guy."

Before the season was over, Vernon also set an American League record for career assists by a first basemen, breaking the old mark of 1,284 held by Washington's Joe Judge. In one of his biggest hits of the season, Mickey's three-run homer beat the Chicago White Sox, 5-4. He also hit the first grand slam of his career in an 18-9 rout of the Boston Red Sox. And he was given a Mercury station wagon by a beer company for being "the most popular Senator."

At the time, Vernon had played in more games than any active player except Enos Slaughter and Phil Cavarretta. "I'd like to play as long as I can," Mickey told Matt Zabitka in an article that appeared in the Chester *Times*.

That fall, Vernon traveled through Pennsylvania, Maryland, and Virginia with a touring team called the Kaline All-Stars. In addition to Al Kaline, the team included Robin Roberts, Gus Triandos, Hal Smith, and Ray Moore. Local teams and sometimes an all-star team from the rapidly deteriorating Negro League provided the opposition.

After the season ended, however, so did Vernon's playing days in Washington. On November 8, he was traded with pitchers Bob Porterfield and Johnny Schmitz and outfielder Tom Umphlet to the Red Sox in a strange deal that brought the Senators pitchers Dick Brodowski, Truman Clevenger, and Al Curtis, and outfielders Neil Chrisley and Karl Olson. Four veterans for five undistinguished players. "Washington took five green sprouts," penned Red Smith.

"It feels kind of funny leaving Washington after so many years," Vernon told reporters. "I'm sincerely sorry to be leaving. It was a second home to me. But now I'm going to an up-and-coming team and I think the Red Sox will win the pennant before long. I sure would like to play in a World Series before I quit."

Boston manager Pinky Higgins was overjoyed at getting Vernon. And he couldn't keep from throwing a barb at the rival Indians. "When the Indians traded Mickey back to Washington in

Boston Red Sox manager Mike Higgins (right) took a look at new players acquired in a trade with the Senators, including (from left) Mickey Vernon, Johnny Schmitz, Tom Umphlet, and Bob Porterfield.

1950, they may have made the worst deal in baseball history," he said. "I figure that Cleveland would have won at least two or three pennants since then if they had Mickey on first base."

Pitcher Mel Parnell, a 21-game winner in 1953, was also elated over the swap. "It was a great day when Boston made that trade because it improved our ballclub in more ways than one," Parnell said. "I was happy to see us get him, not only because of his talent, but because as an individual he was a great team player. "

The Red Sox fielded a lineup that included Ted Williams, Jackie Jensen, Jimmy Piersall, and Billy Goodman. Boston also had first basemen Norm Zauchin and Dick Gernert on the team. Mickey, however, played most of the time, usually batting cleanup behind Williams.

"Pitchers would bear down on Ted and have a tendency to let up on a fellow like me," Vernon said. "This was to my advantage. Also, if they walked him, it opened up a hole for a line drive hitter like me."

There was another advantage to playing with Williams. "It meant I didn't have to field those smacks off his bat anymore," Vernon said.

"I never saw Ted take a bad swing," Mickey added. "He always choked up a little on the bat, but when he got two strikes on him he'd move his hands up a little more."

Playing with Williams was an experience unlike any other Mickey had ever had. And the two become friends and confidants.

"I was as friendly with him as he would let you get," Vernon said. "I didn't go out to dinner with him or anything like that. Our relationship was strictly on the field and in the clubhouse. Unless you were a fisherman, you didn't get that close to him. He talked fishing and hitting. He was always willing to talk hitting with anybody. Away from the ballpark, he pretty much stuck to himself. He was a loner. He had his own room on the road. He usually ate in his room to avoid autograph seekers. But Ted was as well-liked throughout the league as any player I knew. He was very friendly with other players in the league. Of course, he had trouble with some of the writers."

Williams and Vernon were closely linked in two on-field capers that made headlines during the year. One followed Williams's 400th home run of his career.

"He didn't like to shake hands when he crossed the plate, but since I was the next batter, I thought he'd do it this time because it was a special occasion," Vernon said. "But as he approached the plate, he had loaded up his mouth with spit and was making like he was going to unload in the direction of the press box. All I could think about was not getting any of it on me. But he didn't spit. He just made like he was going to do it."

Later, with Mickey again on-deck, Williams did let fly in an act that was intended to punctuate his dislike for the men of the Fourth Estate. As a result of his defiant vulgarity, Williams was fined $5,000.

Another time, Williams came to bat with the bases loaded in the ninth inning of a game against the New York Yankees. With Vernon on deck, the Yanks decided to bring in lefthanded pitcher Tommy Byrne.

"Ted always studied the pitchers very closely," Mickey recalled. "Even when a pitcher was just warming up or a team was bringing in a new pitcher, Ted always moved close to the plate to watch the guy throw. Well, this time he called me over near the plate where he was standing to discuss Byrne. 'Take a look at this guy,' he said. 'What do you think his ball is doing?'"

Byrne, however, didn't appreciate such scrutiny. Almost before Vernon could give Williams an answer, Byrne fired his first warmup pitch at the two batters as they stood about eight feet from the plate. Ted and Mickey ducked. "That flaky, lefthanded bastard," Williams screeched. He then smashed a drive through the middle for a game-winning hit.

It always seemed somewhat ironic that Vernon and Williams broke into the major leagues in the same year (1939), and retired in the same season (1960). Adding to the irony was the fact that Mickey was the first manager of the expansion Washington Senators, and Ted was the team's last pilot in the District of Columbia.

At mid-season, Vernon was again the American League's starting first baseman in the All-Star Game. Mickey compiled 99,560 votes to beat out the Indians' Vic Wertz. Vernon was hitless in two trips to the plate as the National League captured a 7-3 decision.

During one point in the season, Vernon was mired in an 0-for-28 slump. But he countered with some excellent days at the plate. His two-run homer in the seventh inning gave the Red Sox a 6-4 win over the Yankees. He bashed two doubles and a single in a 2-0 win over the Kansas City Athletics. His two-run, ninth-inning homer beat the Athletics, 3-2, in a game in which he also socked two doubles. He had a home run, double, single, and four RBI in a 9-3 win over the Detroit Tigers. The next day, his five RBI with a three-run home run and a single led to an 8-6 victory over the Tigers. Then two days later, he again beat the A's with a two-run homer, 2-1. Over a 14-day stretch, Vernon had 15 RBI with five home runs, five doubles, and five singles.

In 1956, Jackie Robinson, just a little younger than Vernon, was battling injuries and trying to finish what would be his final season. "I wish I felt at 38 as good as Vernon looks," said the Brooklyn Dodgers star. John Carmichael in the Chicago *Daily News* labled Mickey "the ageless wonder."

While Mickey Mantle was winning the batting crown with a .353 average and Williams was finishing second at .345, Vernon wound up with a .310 mark in 119 games. Mickey smacked 15 home runs and collected 84 RBI, which was not too shabby for a guy 38 years old.

Vernon may have been aging, but his bat was still hot as the 1957 season got underway. In a game in which the teams combined for 30 hits, his four RBI, three runs, and three hits helped the Bosox beat Detroit, 11-8. A two-run homer in the eighth beat the Baltimore Orioles, 5-4. Another two-run four-bagger downed Kansas City, 3-2. Then, pinch-hitting with two outs in the bottom of the ninth, Mickey's two-run homer beat the Yankees, 3-2, in a doubleheader in which Vernon also homered in the second game.

All the while, Vernon's co-oldie, Williams, was threatening to hit .400. "You just want to lead the league so you can be the oldest player to do it," Vernon chided the 38-year-old slugger. "No," replied Williams, "I just want to lead the league."

At the end of the season, Williams did indeed lead the league with a .388 average. Vernon, who wound up sharing first base duties with Zauchin and Gernert, hit .241 while playing in just 102 games. The Red Sox jumped to third in the standings.

After the season, Vernon sought some advice from Red Sox general manager Joe Cronin. Mickey told Cronin that he thought he had come to the end of the road and should consider retiring. He said he had been offered a job as a coach with another team. What did Cronin think?

"Don't quit" was Cronin's advice. "Make them cut the uniform off you. You can still hit, and you're in good physical condition. Play as long as you can. Don't walk out because you've had a bad year."

Vernon followed Cronin's recommendation and decided to stay. But that winter, Boston sold him to Cleveland for the $20,000 waiver price. The Red Sox claimed that Mickey "couldn't get the bat around anymore." They'd also acquired Pete Runnels from the Senators to play second base and split first base duties with Gernert (Zauchin was included in the trade for Runnels). Vernon was no longer needed.

"I was totally surprised," Vernon said. "I never thought I might be traded or sold." Although approaching 40, Mickey added that he "hoped to play a few more years."

Detroit had also put in a bid for Vernon, but Cleveland—which also acquired 36-year-old Minnie Minoso in an off-season trade—wanted him more. "His body is more like a 25-year-old than a 40-year-old," said general manager Frankie Lane. "But he's strictly insurance. We got him to give Wertz a lift at first base."

This was one case where insurance really paid off. In spring training, Wertz fractured an ankle sliding into second base in an attempt to break up a double play. He was not expected back until June. Vernon was the Indians' new first baseman.

Vernon took over with a bang. As spring training came to a close, he hit a grand slam home run to help the Indians beat the just-relocated San Francisco Giants in an exhibition game at Corpus Christi, Texas. Then shortly after the season began, he belted another grand slam to lead the Tribe to a 12-2 victory over Jim Bunning and the Tigers. He also smacked a two-run, pinch-hit double with two outs in the ninth to give Jim (Mudcat) Grant his first major league win in a 3-2 Cleveland decision over Kansas City.

After appearing in 17 of the season's first 20 games, Vernon was batting .400 and leading the American League in hitting. As late as June 18, he was still at the top of the circuit with a .380 mark. How was the 40-year-old Vernon doing it?

"He is blessed with robust good health, ageless reflexes, and a figure slim and straight as a foul pole," wrote Neal Eskridge in the Baltimore *News-Post*. Vernon, who as a rookie weighed 170 pounds, was just 15 pounds above that nearly 20 years later.

Mickey never had a weight problem throughout his career.

"I always keep in shape," he told Frank Gibbons of the

Cleveland *Press*. "But I eat what I like and pack away the ice cream. I play a little handball during the winter, and do a few exer cises. But that's all. Once the season starts, I just live. Sleep eight hours a night. Never get into a whirlpool and seldom go on a rubbing table. I never worry about weight. I don't worry about much. There's no tension. If I have a bad game, it may bother me for a while, but I can't say I worry. "

Mickey was still leading the league in hitting with a .349 average when Indians manager Bobby Bragan curiously sent him to the bench and installed 26-year-old Vic Power in the starting lineup. Power was a journeyman player who had made his big league debut with the Philadelphia Athletics in 1954. Cleveland had landed him on June 15 in a five-man trade in which Roger Maris was one of the players sent to Kansas City.

"We're replacing Mickey with a star, not a rookie," Bragan justified. "This is no reflection on Vernon. This just gives us a stronger bench. He can be used in strategic spots."

Even after he was benched, Vernon performed in the All-Star Game. Batting for teammate and pitcher Ray Narleski—whose father, Bill, had played against Mickey back in Delaware County more than 20 years earlier—he singled and scored in what became a 4-3 American League victory. It would be the last of seven All-Star Game appearances for Vernon.

Throughout the rest of the season, Vernon continued to impress those around him. "Both on and off the field, he is the greatest character in the game today," trumpeted Ed McAuley in the Cleveland *News*. "He may be the greatest of all time. His serenity, regardless of the situation, is a wonder to his teammates."

By the end of the season, Vernon was sitting pretty with a .293 batting average. Cleveland, with Bragan having been replaced by Joe Gordon, finished in fourth place despite a lineup that featured veterans such as Robert Avila, Larry Doby, Rocky Colavito, and Minoso.

Again, Vernon appeared in 119 games, making him only the 10th major leaguer since 1900 to play in 100 or more games in one

When Vernon appeared in his 100th game at the age of 40 in 1958, the only active player to have done that was Enos Slaughter (right).

season at the age of 40 or over. Among others in that group were Hall of Famers Honus Wagner, Nap Lajoie, Ty Cobb, Luke Appling, and Slaughter. The 1958 season was the 16th straight in which Mickey had appeared in 100 or more games. By then, he had also broken Lou Gehrig's American League record of having played in 2,143 games at first base.

Little did Vernon realize at the time, though, that his final game of the season with the Indians would be his last one in the American League. After playing in the junior circuit since 1939, Mickey was about to become a National Leaguer.

CHAPTER 14

Mickey and Danny

It would not be accurate to say that they were cut from the same mold.

One was tall and graceful. One was short and bullish. One was easy-going and patient. One was scrappy and aggressive. One was lefthanded. One was righthanded. One came from Marcus Hook. One came from Chester. One was Protestant. One was Catholic.

But despite these differences, Mickey Vernon and Danny Murtaugh were as close as two friends could ever be. Mickey and Danny. Danny and Mickey. Two friends linked inseparably in the annals of Delaware County baseball. In some ways, each one was the brother the other never had.

They had first met as opponents in a church basketball league. A few years later, they became teammates on an American Legion baseball team in Chester. They were 16 years old then. Their lives would be intertwined for the next four decades.

They turned professional the same year, they worked together for a number of years during the off-season, their families got together socially, they played golf together, and they often

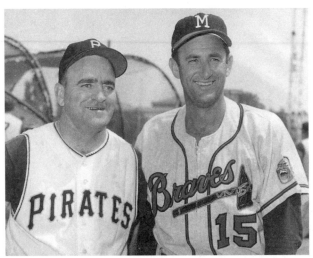

Old friends Danny Murtaugh and Vernon were reunited when
Mickey was traded to the National League's Milwaukee Braves.

appeared jointly on the local banquet circuit. But Vernon and
Murtaugh never played on the same team in the major leagues.

Twice though, they did wear the same uniform. The first time
was in 1960 with the Pittsburgh Pirates. Murtaugh was the manager. Vernon was a coach and a part-time player. The season had
one of the most memorable endings in baseball history.

To reach that point, Vernon had taken an unlikely detour. After
a career-long affiliation with the American League, he had ventured into the National League in 1959. The switch occurred rather
abruptly.

The winter of 1958-59 had been touched by misfortunate for
Mickey. While driving in Chester, he was involved in a five-car
accident at Providence Road and 25th Street. A bus had stopped
suddenly going down the hill on Providence. That set off a chain
reaction with a car hitting the bus, then Mickey hitting that car,
getting rear-ended by a fourth car, which in turn was hit by a fifth
auto that had run a red light at 25th Street.

The only one injured in the crash was Vernon. He suffered face
cuts and a bruised knee, and was treated on the spot by a doctor
who was passing by. Mickey's Volkswagen was totaled.

In a sharp reversal of previous years, Vernon signed his contract with Cleveland in January. Recovered from his auto injuries, he reported to spring training in excellent condition. Later, he got several key hits in late-season exhibition games in Des Moines and Omaha.

Vernon opened the campaign with the Indians, but on April 11 in Kansas City, manager Joe Gordon stopped him on the way to the clubhouse after the second game of the season. Putting his arm around Vernon's shoulders, Gordon, an old friend of Mickey's, said: "Hey buddy, you've just been traded."

It wasn't the kind of news Mickey expected to hear. He had been traded to the Milwaukee Braves for pitcher Humberto Robinson. "If it hadn't been to Milwaukee, I wouldn't have gone," said Vernon. "But they'd just won two pennants and I thought they had a chance at another one." The Braves had a potent line-up that featured Hank Aaron, Eddie Mathews, Bill Bruton, Frank Torre, Joe Adcock, and Wes Covington. Warren Spahn, Lew Burdette, and Bob Buhl led a powerful pitching staff.

"They had great hitting and great pitching," Vernon said. "But they had two weak spots. Left field and second base. That was the year Red Schoendienst was out for the whole season with tuberculosis."

It was reported that the Phillies had offered pitcher Robin Roberts to the Indians for Mickey and a pitcher. But the deal fell through when the Indians wouldn't add the unnamed hurler to the swap. Nevertheless, Vernon had suddenly become a National Leaguer for the first time.

Although he hadn't played since an April 1 exhibition game, Vernon didn't waste any time making his presence felt. In the Braves' home opener against none other than the Phillies, he drew a pinch-hit walk batting for Felix Mantilla in the seventh inning. He stayed in the game and in the ninth he singled off Dick Farrell to drive in Johnny Logan, who had doubled, to pull Milwaukee to a 3-3 tie. Then former Seattle University All-American basketball player Johnny O'Brien, just traded by the Phillies, slapped a 10th inning single that gave the Braves a 4-3 victory.

At spring training, the nattily attired Mickey pointed out the sights to Lib and Gay.

The losing pitcher in the game was Dick Farrell. Later that night in his hotel room, Farrell was still sufficiently irritated that when he looked into a mirror and saw himself, he punched the mirror. The blow rewarded Farrell with a broken pitching hand. He was subsequently fined by Phils manager Eddie Sawyer.

Adjusting to the pitching in a different league is never easy, and Vernon had to learn a whole new process. "It was a big adjustment," he said. "I had to learn all new pitchers. I wasn't playing every day, so that made it tougher. And after a while, I realized that National League umpires called low pitches more than American League umpires."

In late May, Vernon was a witness to one of the two greatest games ever pitched (the other being Don Larsen's perfect game in the 1956 World Series). It was the game in which Harvey Haddix of the Pirates pitched a perfect game against the Braves for 12 innings, then lost in the 13th on a controversial hit by Adcock.

"Haddix wasn't overpowering," Vernon said, "but he turned

the ball over well, and he was getting us out. While he was pitching, there wasn't much conversation on our bench. We just went about our business, figuring we'd get to him eventually."

With Mantilla on second after breaking up the perfect game by reaching base on an error, and Hank Aaron, having been intentionally walked on first, Adcock blasted a pitch over the right field fence. While Mantilla scored on the hit, Aaron, thinking the ball had hit the wall, touched second then trotted back to the dugout figuring that the winning run had scored. Meanwhile, Adcock was eventually ruled out for technically passing Aaron on the basepath. He was denied a home run, credited with a double, and the Braves were awarded a 1-0 victory.

"After the game, Adcock was moaning and groaning in the shower about losing a home run," Vernon recalled. "Aaron said, 'I'll hit one tomorrow and you can have it.'"

Braves manager Fred Haney insisted that the 41-year-old Vernon would be "strictly a pinch-hitter," but he changed his mind in June after Covington, the regular left fielder, got hurt. First baseman Joe Adcock didn't want to move to the outfield. Haney asked Mickey to play left. Although he hadn't played in the outfield since his days in the Navy, Vernon obliged.

In his first game in left, Vernon, joining Bill Bruton in center and Hank Aaron in right, singled and scored in the second inning, and smacked a three-run homer in the third to lead the Braves to a 7-6 decision over the Los Angeles Dodgers. "Defensively, though, I wasn't familiar with the position, so I had a few problems," Vernon said. "A few games later, I had to run to the left field line for a ball, and I dropped it."

As it turned out, Vernon played only four games in the outfield. Then he returned to his previous role as a pinch-hitter. In a September game, Mickey's two-out, pinch-hit single off Roberts in the top of the ninth helped the Braves to an 8-5 win over the Phillies at Connie Mack Stadium.

By the end of the season, Vernon had played in 74 games, including 10 at first base. He had hit two pinch-hit home runs—

one off Stu Miller and the San Francisco Giants, the other off Dave Hillman and the Chicago Cubs—the only pinch-hit round-trippers in his career. Mickey finished with a .220 batting average.

As Mickey had hoped, Milwaukee had a shot at the World Series. The Braves and Dodgers finished the season tied for first place. In a best-of-three playoff, however, the Braves lost the first two games, thus yielding a spot in the Fall Classic to LA.

After the season, Vernon was released. It looked like his playing career had ended. And his chance to get into a World Series was virtually dead. Neither, however, was the case.

Enter Danny Murtaugh.

Murtaugh grew up in Chester, and while attending Chester High School, had played with Vernon on a local American Legion team. But after they joined the professional ranks, the paths of Murtaugh and Vernon had often come close, but never quite overlapped.

The two broke into pro ball together in 1937, playing for Easton and Cambridge, respectively, in the Eastern Shore League. Once when the teams met, Murtaugh struck out in a key situation, then made an error. A fan spewed verbal abuse in Danny's direction. But he suddenly changed course after Mickey fanned with the bases loaded. Vernon became his target.

Mickey was getting pretty annoyed, so he yelled to the guy, "Come on down here." He came down to the fence, and stood about six-foot, six. Vernon yelled out, "Hey Danny, I got him down here for you."

While Mickey moved up the following year, Danny stayed another season at Cambridge before starting his own climb up the ladder. In 1941, he began the season with Houston in the Texas League, but in June, Murtaugh landed with the Phillies, and in 85 games led the National League in stolen bases with 18. He spent the next two years as the Phillies regular second baseman before entering military service in 1944

Danny also played with the Boston Braves and Pirates. In 1949, he and Vernon hit home runs on the same day—the only time that ever happened to them. In an added piece of irony, each homer came against the old hometown teams Murtaugh's against the Phillies and Vernon's against the Athletics.

During the off-season through much of their playing days, Vernon and Murtaugh worked out together and played handball against each other at the Chester YMCA. The two often attended banquets together at different spots around Delaware County. They played golf together, often getting joined by pitcher Tom Ferrick, a resident of nearby Havertown. And their families socialized frequently, sometimes at the Vernon home in Wallingford, sometimes at the Murtaugh residence in Woodlyn.

As ballplayers in those days had to do to pay their bills, they had jobs during the off-season. Danny had originally worked at Sears in downtown Chester, but after Mickey got a job at McGovern's, a men's clothing store also in Chester, he joined him there. Hired primarily for their promotional value, the two sold mostly suits for a number of years.

For years, Murtaugh and Vernon had shared a friendly pact. Whoever becomes a manager first, they agreed, will hire the other as a coach.

Murtaugh had taken over the reins of the Pittsburgh Pirates during the 1957 season while Vernon was still playing. Danny had left the big leagues as a player after the 1951 season, then had managed for four years in the minors before becoming a coach with the Bucs in 1956. On August 3 the following year, he replaced Bobby Bragan as the Pirates' pilot.

Nearly as soon as Mickey was discharged by the Braves after the 1959 campaign, Danny jumped in. He offered Vernon a job as his first base coach. Mickey, however, wasn't sure his playing days were over. The New York Yankees had an interest in signing him as a backup first baseman. He was in New York to talk with club officials when Murtaugh called. "I have to know if you want the job or not," he said.

Vernon never made it to the interview. Instead, he accepted Murtaugh's offer, and returned right away to Wallingford to meet

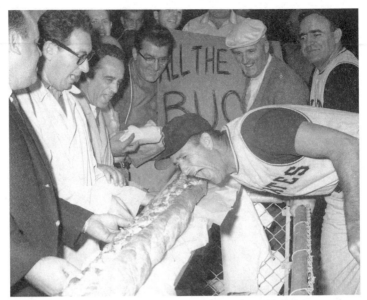

Together for the first time in their pro careers in 1960, Mickey and
Danny tasted a giant hoagie delivered to the ballpark by their friends
from Delaware County.

with his old friend. The 1960 season would mark the first time the
two had been members of the same team since those days long ago
with the Chester Legion team. It was a happy reunion.

"They admired each other tremendously," said Danny's son
Tim, who played himself in the minors before managing for seven
years, advancing as high as the Columbus (Ohio) Red Birds in the
International League. "They came from different backgrounds,
but they were always very good friends. Dad thought that Mickey
brought a lot to the table, which is why he hired him. He didn't
just do it because they were friends.

"Later, when Mickey managed in Washington, my dad
thought he was an outstanding manager. He said that if Mickey
had been with a better team, he would've been very successful.
My dad had great respect for Mickey's baseball mind. He knew
the game inside and out."

"We didn't let our friendship interfere with our jobs," Vernon
said. "The players realized our relationship, but we didn't flaunt

it. But it was a great thrill for me to work with Danny. I learned more from him than from any other manager I worked with."

As a coach with the Pirates, one of Vernon's special duties was to work with first baseman Dick Stuart. A guy who had power to burn, Stuart was a terrible fielder who picked up nicknames such as Dr. Strangeglove and Stonehands. Later, when he joined the Phillies, Stuart once chastised pitcher Jim Bunning because his pickoff throws to first were coming in too hard.

"Mickey worked with Stuart, and made him a better fielder," said Tim Murtaugh. "Or maybe I should say, less bad."

Another side of Vernon was revealed when he was in Pittsburgh. "I only got ejected four times in my life from a big league game, but one of them came when I was a coach with the Pirates," he said.

Umpire Ken Burkhart called the Pirates' Roberto Clemente out at first on a close play during an outing with the Phillies at Connie Mack Stadium. Vernon said he was safe. "Get back in the coaching box," Burkhart odered. "If you don't you're gone." A few innings later, Pittsburgh pitcher Bob Friend reached base, and when the batboy delivered his warmup jacket, Mickey stepped over to the bag to help him put it on. "I told you not to step out of the box," said Burkhart, a former big league pitcher. "You're gone."

When Murtaugh became manager in 1957, the Pirates were floundering, and despite playing a little over .500 ball after Danny took over, finished tied with the Cubs for seventh place. The following year, however, the club soared all the way to second, placing eight games behind the Braves. Then in 1959, Pittsburgh tumbled back to fourth, but finished just nine games out of first.

By 1960, the Pirates had put together a talented team that featured Clemente, Dick Groat, Bill Mazeroski, Don Hoak, Bill Virdon, Bob Skinner, Stuart, and Smoky Burgess on the starting eight. The pitching staff was headed by Friend, Vern Law, and Elroy Face.

Late in the season, however, with injuries taking a toll, the Pirates came down with a shortage of pinch-hitters. Vernon was summoned to active duty. At 42, he was the oldest active player in the National League.

Mickey came to bat just eight times and managed one hit. It came off the Braves Ron Piche. In the final at-bat of his career on September 27, Mickey grounded out to Eddie Kasko with one out in the 11th inning in a 4-3 Pirates victory over the Cincinnati Reds in 16 innings.

But he did gain a place in baseball history by becoming one of the rare players who performed in the majors in four decades. Only a handful of others—Eddie Collins, Ted Williams, Early Wynn, Tim McCarver, Willie McCovey, Jim Kaat, Nolan Ryan (Minnie Minoso doesn't count)—have lasted that long.

Naturally, the highlight of Vernon's tenure with the Bucs—like everyone else's in Pittsburgh—came in the World Series that year. The Pirates had captured their first National League pennant since 1927, cruising home seven games ahead of the Braves. For Vernon, that meant he had reached a level that had previously been denied him in 20 years in the big leagues.

"So many other times, I just missed," Vernon remembered. "I got to Cleveland the year after it won a pennant. I played in Milwaukee the year after the Braves had won two straight pennants. You play all those years, but never quite make it. But this time, I finally did."

In an incredibly bizarre World Series against the Yankees, the Bucs won three games by the grand total of six runs (6-4, 3-2, 5-2), while losing three by scores of 16-3, 10-0, and 12-0.

The Series came down to the final game at Forbes Field in Pittsburgh. In a game as strange as the results of the previous six, the Pirates built a 4-0 lead in the second inning, only to fall behind 5-4 in the sixth. The Yanks stretched their lead to 7-4 in the eighth, but Hal Smith's three-run homer in the bottom half capped a five-run Pittsburgh comeback that put the Bucs ahead, 9-7. That lead vanished in the ninth as New York pulled to a 9-9 tie.

That set the stage for Bill Mazeroski. Leading off the bottom of the ninth against Ralph Terry, the Pirates' second baseman

The vocal side of Vernon was on display as he engaged in a heated debate with umpire Al Barlick after a close call at first base.

launched a 1-0 fastball over the left-center field wall for a game and Series-winning home run. The blast is generally regarded as the most memorable home run ever hit in a baseball game.

At first base, Vernon, who was ineligible for the Series as a player, was the first person to congratulate Mazeroski as he circled the bases. Then Mickey dashed to home plate where he joined a raucous celebration that engulfed the homer-hitting hero.

"It was one of my greatest thrills," Vernon said. "I just don't have any words to describe what it was like on the field when you win a game like that. When I saw the ball go out, I was just so charged up. We all were. I've never had an experience like it."

Just around the corner, Vernon faced another new experience.

Becoming a Manager

For 60 years beginning in 1901 the number of major league baseball teams never varied. There were eight teams in the American League, and there were eight teams in the National League.

Before the birth of the American League in the year following the start of the 20th century, there had been no set format. The National League, originated in 1876, had carried as many as 12 teams and as few as six. Other alliances that were considered major leagues—most notably the National Association, which existed between 1871 and 1875, and the American Association, which ran from 1882 to 1891—also had varying numbers of teams.

Franchises, of course, had switched cities during those 60 years, especially in the 1950s when teams in places such as Boston, St. Louis, Philadelphia, Brooklyn, and New York moved to what were perceived as greener pastures. But for six full decades, there was no fluctuation in the number of teams that played in the major leagues.

That all changed in 1961. It was the year that expansion came to the big leagues.

In the previous 15 years dating back to 1946, the Senators had managed to escape the second division just once. They had finished in last place five times and in seventh four times. With dwindling crowds and a deteriorating ballpark, the Nats were a team going nowhere fast. "Washington didn't have very good ballclubs during that time," said Sam Mele, who spent most of his career with the Senators and Boston Red Sox. "The team didn't have many fans, and it couldn't pay big salaries. One year I knocked in 94 runs and had to argue like mad to get a little raise."

For four years in the late 1950s, Calvin Griffith, the adopted son of Washington Senators owner Clark Griffith, who had died in 1955, had tried to move the struggling team he now ran. His first choice was to Los Angeles, but he was beaten to the punch by the Dodgers and Walter O'Malley. He then focused on Minneapolis-St. Paul, a significantly untapped area of the Upper Midwest.

Repeatedly, however, Griffith's plan had been thwarted by the hierarchy that ran the American League. Having no team in the Nation's Capital was simply unthinkable, they reasoned. Moreover, with baseball then in the midst of Congressional hearings involving anti-trust laws, it was not a prudent time to incur the wrath of the politicians.

Such logic notwithstanding, it was therefore wholly perplexing when on October 26, 1960 the American League made a stunning announcement. The Senators, it was disclosed, were moving to Minnesota—ironically where they would be managed by Mele—and new teams would be established in Washington and Los Angeles, increasing the number of clubs in the league to 10. The reconstituted league would be launched the following season. (Earlier, the National League had announced that new teams would be located in New York and Houston, beginning in 1962.)

As it turned out, the American League, led by its president Joe Cronin, a former Senators player and Calvin Griffith's brother-in-law, had brokered a "New Deal" with Washington. The old Senators team would be forgiven for becoming the Minnesota

Twins if a new Senators team replaced it in Washington. Consider it done.

Three weeks after the announcement, Cronin introduced the new Senators' owners. Members of the group, each of whom had reportedly invested between $500,000 and $750,000, included a former ambassador to Ireland, heads of the Glenn L. Martin and the Hecht companies, a collection of investment bankers and attorneys, and Katherine Graham, the wife of the publisher of the Washington *Post.* President of the group was Lt. General Elwood

Managing was a new experience for Vernon when he became the expansion Senators' first pilot.

(Pete) Quesada, the director of the Federal Aviation Agency and a highly decorated veteran of World War II who had flown 90 combat missions and directed the Ninth Tactical Bombing Command in England. Quesada was a native Washingtonian, and a long-time friend of Cronin's.

On November 19, two days after the ownership group was revealed, the team's top two baseball people were named. Ed Doherty, the president of the minor league American Association for the previous eight years, was the general manager. And a guy named Mickey Vernon was the manager.

Vernon, of course, had never managed before. But he was one of the most popular players ever to wear the uniform of the old Senators, so his appointment was overwhelmingly logical from a public relations standpoint, and, like the arrival of the new team, it was greeted in Washington with considerable applause.

"The Senators have picked the nicest guy since Walter Johnson," proclaimed Shirley Povich in the Washington *Post*. Elsewhere, others were just as delighted. "This is a wonderful opportunity for Mickey. He has the potential to be a real good manager," Danny Murtaugh told Ed Gebhart in the Delaware County *Daily Times*. And Arthur Daley, writing in the New York *Times*, commented, "Even if he doesn't talk much, he observes and is smart enough to have learned plenty."

In a way, though, it was a strange choice. "Managing was never one of my dreams," Vernon said many years later. "I had never even thought about it as a player. I had no great desire to manage."

The job offer had originally taken shape during the 1960 World Series while Vernon was a coach with the Pittsburgh Pirates. Before one of the games, Vernon had walked over to the box seats to say hello to Cronin's wife, Mildred, the sister of Calvin Griffith. During the conversation, she told Mickey that an expansion team was coming to Washington. "Have you ever thought about managing?" she asked. "No, not really," was his reply.

Nevertheless, that winter Vernon received a telephone call from Murtaugh, who'd just. been contacted by Quesada asking permission to talk with Mickey. "How'd you like to manage a ball club?" Danny inquired. "What is this, a riddle?" a skeptical Vernon responded. "Quit pulling my leg."

Murtaugh told Vernon, "Call this number." A few minutes later, when he did, Mickey found out that he was dialing Cronin's private number and that Quesada was in the office waiting to make his pitch. The pitch was straight down the middle: Quesada wanted Vernon as his manager, and there were no other candidates for the job.

Vernon, who ironically had applied the year before for a coaching job with the now-departed Senators, drove to the Nation's Capital, signed a two-year contract for a reported $25,000 per year, and shortly afterward, to the surprise of most Washington watchers, was introduced as the first manager of the new expansion Senators.

One of Mickey's coaches with the Senators was his former team-mate and close friend George Case.

"I'm tickled to death," Mickey said at the press conference. "Every fellow in this game aspires to be a big league manager. I am surprised and delighted that I was chosen."

Vernon said he accepted the job because "you never know if you are going to get the chance again."

"I have been an admirer of Mickey Vernon since I was a little boy," added Quesada.

Once the niceties were over, the real work began. First on the agenda was to name a coaching staff. Vernon chose former teammates and two of his best friends, George Case and Sid Hudson, as well as veteran baseball journeyman George Susce. A coach at Cleveland when Mickey was with the Indians, Susce was put in charge of the bullpen. A fourth coach, Rollie Hemsley, was added by management to the staff as the team's first base coach.

Case, a stellar outfielder with the Senators from 1937 through 1945 and again in 1947, was an excellent hitter who was regarded as one of the fastest runners in baseball. He had led the

American League in stolen bases six times (including one year when he was with the Cleveland Indians), and had once taken on Olympic sprinter Jesse Owens in an exhibition race.

By 1960, Case had become the owner of a successful sporting goods store in Trenton, New Jersey. He was also the head baseball coach at Rutgers University. Case gave up both jobs to become Vernon's third base coach in Washington.

Likewise, Hudson relinquished his job as a scout with the Boston Red Sox to take a post as the Senators' pitching coach. One of the American League's top hurlers during a big league career that ran from 1940 to 1954, he had won 40 games in his first three years in the majors.

"I liked that job better than any I ever had in baseball," recalled Hudson, whose career as a pro and college pitching coach extended into the 1990s. "Mickey would ask your advice. He relied on you. A lot of managers don't do that."

Vernon's hiring of Case and Hudson was not only a reunion for the three men, it also brought together their families. "Lib, Marian Hudson, and my mother, Helen, had always been very friendly," remembered George Case Jr. "They were all excited to be back in Washington together. Plus, the Vernons' daughter, Gay, was the same age as my sister, Robin, and the Hudsons had two girls who were also the same age. So it was a great time for all of the families."

For the men, though, an extremely difficult task faced them. They had to assemble a ball club from scratch. The players would come mostly from a pool of players selected from other teams.

Prior to the draft, the Senators signed veteran infielder Danny O'Connell as a free agent, and acquired two minor league pitchers at the winter meetings in Louisville, Kentucky. For the draft itself, each American League team was required to submit a list of 15 available players from its roster. Both the Senators and the other expansion entry, the Los Angeles Angels, a team owned by cowboy singer/actor Gene Autry, were allowed to select 28 players, paying $75,000 apiece for them.

The draft was scheduled to be held on December 13 in Cronin's office in Boston. Because of a raging snowstorm, the draft was postponed one day. Driving to Boston, the Washington group arrived well behind the Los Angeles contingent, headed by general manager Fred Haney and manager Bill Rigney. Once it began, the draft took seven hours to complete.

While the Angels seemed to focus more on acquiring young players—for instance, getting 19-year-old shortstop Jim Fregosi and a number of youthful pitchers, including Dean Chance—both teams went heavily for veterans. LA chose well-seasoned players such as Eddie Yost, Ted Kluszewski, Leon Wagner, Steve Bilko, Albie Pearson, and Joe Koppe. Washington, which Vernon later revealed, "didn't have a lot of good information on the younger players," grabbed aging veterans such as Gene Woodling, Dale Long, Willie Tasby, and Billy Klaus, and pitchers Dick Donovan, Bobby Shantz, and Tom Sturdivant.

Neither team's selections impressed anybody. That feeling was portrayed by Philadelphia *Evening Bulletin* columnist Sandy Grady when he wrote that the two clubs "were burdened with $2,100,000 worth of spongy arms, varicose veins, and dead bats."

Especially chastised were the Senators' choices. "The baseball punjabs tittered that the Senators were the funniest thing since Bill Veeck's midget—except the midget would outhit them," Grady wrote. He added, "They are unique in that almost every bloke is a discard. These are the major leagues' unwanted, the outsiders, the junked machinery."

Said Branch Rickey, the highly esteemed former baseball executive, "I wouldn't be surprised if the Senators were forced to withdraw from the American League by May 15."

To that, Vernon replied, "I didn't take this job with the intention of finishing last. I'd say my job is more an opportunity than a challenge."

It was certainly a challenge. Probably the Senators' best player was the 39-year-old Woodling, who had played in the Navy with Vernon more than 17 years earlier. He was also the highest-paid player, earning a salary of $34,000. Long, another "name" player was 35 years old, while Donovan, projected as the top pitcher, was 34.

Shortly after the draft was completed, Washington picked three more minor league players for $25,000 apiece. Two days later, the club made its first trade. It sent Shantz, its first pick in the draft, to the Pirates for pitcher Bennie Daniels, third baseman Harry Bright, and first baseman R.C. Stevens. The deal had been consummated at McGovern's men's store in Chester where both Vernon and Murtaugh were working that winter. "We discussed and haggled back and forth between sales," Vernon said.

In January, the Senators made a number of other moves. Hal Keller, who'd played in just 25 games as a major leaguer a decade earlier and was the brother of former New York Yankees outfielder Charlie, was named farm director. Cronin's son, Tommy, was appointed assistant farm director. The team signed a one-year lease to play at Griffith Stadium. Season tickets met with an enthusiastic response when they went on sale. And a board of directors was named with Quesada leaving his job with the FAA to become the team's full-time president.

By the time spring training opened at Pompano Beach, Florida, the Senators had added to their collection of veterans, bringing the number of players in camp to 35. The team, however, had no farm system, and had to send young players to the minor league camps of other big league clubs. And even Vernon was unfamiliar with many of the players on the roster. On his first day on the job, he went around introducing himself and shaking hands with all the players. One of those he greeted as a player turned out to be the club's laundryman.

Vernon, though, was optimistic about the team's chances for the 1961 season. "Everybody picks us for last," he told Grady, who had taken a particular interest in the manager from Marcus Hook. "They say that beating Los Angeles for ninth place will be an achievement. But I keep thinking of what a new chance on a ball club does for a player sometimes. A lot of these fellows could prove everybody wrong. I know I'm a little surprised how eager, how hopped-up and happy they all seem."

"There will be triumphs and there will be disappointments for the fledgling Nats this season," penned Bob Addie in the Washington *Post*. "But they've already accomplished one minor miracle by existing at all."

Aside from the team's roster and projected rank in the standings, one of the other big questions concerned Mickey himself. What kind of manager would this quiet, unassuming gentleman be? Without managerial experience, could he put together a team with some semblance of ability? And having been in the National League for the last two years, how much did he now know about the American League?

Vernon supplied some answers. "I never managed," he told the *Evening Bulletin's* Ray Kelly. "So I can't really say what I'm going to do. But I'll tell you this: If I have to get tough, I'll get tough. Nobody is going to run over me.

"I've worked for nine different managers, and I should have learned something from people like Bucky Harris, Lou Boudreau, Charlie Dressen, Fred Haney, Bobby Bragan, Joe Kuehl, and Ossie Bluege," he added. "And I learned a lot more when I coached for Murtaugh at Pittsburgh last season."

The *Post's* Povich also probed the question. "The manager has to get along with 25 players," Vernon told him. "That will be strictly my problem. Everybody says I'm an easy-going fellow. They may not be doing me any favors. I hate bad baseball, and I've already told my gang I will be very disagreeable if they don't give me all the good baseball they've got."

Vernon added that he once heard Harris say that a manager's biggest problem was knowing when to change pitchers. "Everybody can pick a starting pitcher," Harris had said. "How long you let him go is the big decision."

Matt Zabitka, writing in *The Sporting News*, also drew a bead on Vernon's expected managerial style. "It's no secret that I'm not what you'd label a vociferous guy or of the blood and guts

In his first game as Senators' manager, Vernon met before the first pitch with umpires and White Sox skipper Al Lopez.

school," Vernon said. "And I'm certainly not going to change overnight for the sake of showboating and become somebody I'm not. I'll be the same guy I was last year, and the year before. Believe me, I'm no softie. By the same token, I don't believe in running a ball club with a whip. Let's say that I plan to use tact in running the team with the accent more on sugar than vinegar. If a player produces, he has nothing to worry about."

Adding to the chorus of those dissecting Vernon's forthcoming technique as a skipper was Arthur Richman of the New York *Mirror*. Would the players take advantage of Mickey's good nature? "I'm not exactly stupid," Vernon replied. "This is my livelihood, and I can get mighty tough with anyone who tries to make a monkey of me. I haven't been around all these years for nothing. I think I know most of the tricks."

Mickey said that he considered the Senators' strong point would be their outfield. The pitching staff was adequate, too. But the club was weak at catcher, desperately needed a good double play combination, and the bench was suspect. Regardless, Vernon said he thought that his team could not only finish ahead of the Angels, but could be better than a couple of other clubs, too.

As spring training drew to a close, it was time to start finding out if that assumption had any merit.

CHAPTER 16

Skipper of the Senators

It had rained the night before. And the weather was damp and cold with the temperature just reaching into the high 40s. But in Washington, D.C., it was a perfect day for a ball game.

The date was April 10, 1961. Opening Day at Griffith Stadium. The Washington Senators versus the Chicago White Sox in the traditional game that launched each year's major league baseball season.

Washington had been anxiously awaiting the date for six months. Following the 1960 season, the team that had been the Washington Senators for 60 years had become the Minnesota Twins. It had been replaced by an "expansion team" also called the Washington Senators. Now, after a winter and spring of preparation, the day to put the new team on the field had finally arrived.

High expectations were the order of the day. Excitement reigned. Newspapers were choked with articles about the new kids in town. And fans demonstrated a level of interest that hadn't been directed toward a baseball team in Washington since perhaps the 1930s.

President John F. Kennedy was joined by Vernon and American League
president Joe Cronin (center) when he threw out the first ball in 1963.

"You can't imagine the level of excitement," said Chuck
Hinton, at the time a highly promising rookie outfielder drafted by
the Senators out of the Baltimore Orioles' system. "Everybody was
sky high. And that carried over to the players. We were all raring
to go, both the younger guys as well as the older guys."

Some 26,725 fans, a little less than 700 below the capacity of
Griffith Stadium, were in attendance as Vice President Lyndon B.
Johnson led a parade of dignitaries to center field to raise the
American flag. President John F. Kennedy, wearing no overcoat
despite the weather, then threw out the first ball. It sailed over the
heads of the players assembled near Kennedy and into the waiting
hands of Chicago's Jim Rivera. As was the custom, the White Sox
outfielder promptly stepped to the presidential box to get the chief
executive's signature on his newly secured treasure.

Minutes later, Dick Donovan took the mound for the Senators.
Ironically, his opponent on the rubber was none other than old
Washington ace Early Wynn, a close friend and former roommate
of Senators manager Mickey Vernon.

For Vernon, it would be the start of a long, hard journey as the
molder of the new Senators' fortunes. Since becoming the team's

manager, he had been analyzed and reanalyzed throughout the off-season. He had patiently answered all the questions, both the honest and the inane ones. And, to his everlasting credit, he had resisted the temptation to admit that he might have been dealt a very bad hand by the chief architects of the Washington roster.

"They gave him hardly anything," recalled Russ White, who in 1961 was a young writer with the Washington *Daily News.* "It was brutal. They didn't draft very wisely, they didn't spend any money, and they ended up with a pretty wretched team. There were old players at almost every position. The Washington Senators never had a worse club. It was dismal in almost all aspects. "

The Senators' first lineup read like a cross between "whatever happened to so-and-so?" and "who is this guy, anyway?" Shortstop Coot Veal led off, followed by Billy Klaus at third base, Marty Keough in right field, Dale Long at first base, Gene Woodling in left field, Willie Tasby in center, Danny O'Connell at second, and Pete Daley catching.

The lineup, however, could have passed for that of a pennant-contender in the early stages as the Senators knocked Wynn out of the box in two innings while taking a 3-0 lead. But the White Sox, with the help of a solo homer by former Senator Roy Sievers, pulled to a 3-3 tie in the eighth. Then in the ninth, Minnie Minoso was hit by a pitch, stole second, went to third on a throwing error by Daley, and scored on Sievers' sacrifice fly. That gave Chicago a 4-3 victory and spoiled a glittering performance by Donovan, who allowed just six hits and one earned run in nine innings of work.

Still, it was not a bad opening for a team that had been almost unanimously sentenced to a season without parole from the bottom of the American League standings. And the best was yet to come.

Astonishingly, the Senators won 17 of their first 39 games, and after 60 games sat proudly with a 30-30 record. At one point, Washington even swept a doubleheader with the New York Yankees behind the pitching of Donovan and Bennie Daniels. Was this a mirage or what?

"Pitching is the key," the grizzled Woodling told Sandy Grady of the Philadelphia *Evening Bulletin*. "But this whole club acts tough. They know they're the guys baseball didn't want. The other night after we lost to Detroit, a writer called us the worst team in baseball. So we got a little hot and knocked off the Tigers twice. This is the Foreign Legion of baseball—deadend guys with nothing to lose and a lot to gain."

Adding to the euphoria, seven buses carrying some 300 fans from Delaware County traveled to Washington to honor Vernon. "About then, I was feeling great," Mickey recalled. "Here I was managing only two years after I was an active player. I had been looking forward to staying in the game in some capacity, but I never thought I'd be a manager that soon."

Even the hard-to-please Quesada applauded his own managerial choice. "Mickey Vernon has a pleasant side which is predominant," he said. "But it's accompanied by a reasonable force resulting in a superior personality."

In mid-June, the Senators visited Boston for a four-game series at Fenway Park. Unfortunately, the bubble was about to burst. Washington had leads in all four games, and blew each one in the late innings. The low point came when a grand slam homer by Jim Paglioroni fueled a Red Sox comeback that overcame a 12-5 Senators' lead.

"It was all downhill after that," Vernon recalled. "The players tried. But a lot of them had their best days behind them."

Washington won just 31 of its final 101 games, and finished the season tied for ninth place with the Kansas City Athletics with a 61-100 record. They trailed the first place New York Yankees by 47½ games. Meanwhile, the expansion Los Angeles Angels placed eighth with a 70-91 mark, nine games above the Nats and A's.

The Senators were not without a few bright spots. Donovan (10-10) led the league with a 2.40 earned run average. Daniels had a 12-11 mark. Woodling, reduced mostly to a part-time role, hit .313, while catcher Gene Green hit .280. Green poled 18 home runs, and Long and Tasby each hit 17. And O'Connell played a good

Vernon stayed on top of the action as he watched from the front of the dugout.

season at shortstop after moving there to make room for young Chuck Cottier, acquired during the season to play second.

"The team was made up of a bunch of young guys just coming up, and a lot of older guys who were borderline players," recalled Cottier, who went on to play nine years in the majors before becoming manager of the Seattle Mariners and later a big league coach and scout. "Mickey just let them play. He gave you every chance to prove what you could do. He expected you to be ready. It's just too bad all the players didn't step up and give him what we should have."

"It was hard managing a team like that," Vernon remembered. "A lot of veteran players were hoping to get swapped before the trading deadline, but when they weren't, they let down after that." In many cases, the merits of that view were reflected in the club's stats.

As a team, the Senators placed last in the league in batting and eighth in fielding. They scored the fewest runs of any American League club. But under the solid guidance of Hudson, the pitching staff had the sixth best ERA in the circuit, and allowed fewer runs than four other teams.

After the season, Vernon returned to Wallingford to contemplate the ordeal he had just experienced. Helping him put his thoughts together was a new part-time job writing a weekly column for the Associated Press.

Although Mickey was never the most talkative guy with the media, he had always gotten along well with the members of the Fourth Estate. As a manager, that didn't change.

"When I started covering baseball as a 23-year-old kid," said Dick Heller, who began his career with the Washington *Evening Star*, "Mickey was still playing. He went out of his way to be nice and accommodating to me. A lot of the players were strictly mediocre. But Mickey and Eddie Yost were really helpful. Mickey was still that way as a manager."

As a result, Vernon was treated well by the Washington press, despite his team's poor showing on the field. "Because of Mickey, you couldn't knock the team," White said. "No one was going to attack Mickey Vernon."

Shortly after the 1961 season ended, the Senators had given themselves what they thought would be a major boost to the lineup—as well as a much-needed drawing card—when they acquired outfielder Jimmy Piersall in a trade with the Cleveland Indians. To get the veteran flychaser, though, the Nats had to pay a high price, surrendering Donovan, Green, infielder Jim Mahoney, and a player to be named later.

The addition of Piersall, plus the emergence of good young players such as Hinton, Cottier, Harry Bright, and Bob Johnson, built Vernon's confidence as the 1962 spring training approached. "I don't know about the A's," Mickey said to the Philadelphia *Evening Bulletin's* Ed Pollack, but I'm confident we won't finish last. We didn't last year, and that surprised a lot of people. With what we have now, we should do even better than a tie for ninth."

Still, Vernon confessed, the Nats lacked power, front-line pitching, and adequate catching. One thing the team didn't lack, though, was a manager who the players thoroughly liked and respected.

One of the Senators' top prospects when he joined the club was 19-year-old infielder Eddie Brinkman (left).

"He was a player's manager," Cottier said. "He didn't have a lot of team meetings. No threatening policies like a lot of managers have. When you were around him, he made you feel important. He'd listen to you, then try to help you. I remember in my first year with him I was single and a little out of control. Mickey gave me some advice. 'Please come back married,' he said. 'It will make you a better player.' And he was right.

"His personality and character carried over into his managerial skills," Cottier added. "He was always professional. He had class. Good manners. Always dressed well. One of the things that really stood out was his patience. He didn't rush into things. His attitude was, you're a big leaguer, act like a big leaguer, play like a big leaguer. A lot of managers with Mickey's characteristics are taken advantage of. No one tried that with Mickey. We had too much respect for him."

Late in the 1961 season, the Senators had brought up a 19-year-old shortstop named Eddie Brinkman. Although he was considered to have a high ceiling, Brinkman was in awe of his surroundings. Vernon, he recalled, played a major role in helping him to bridge the gap from the low minors to the majors.

"I was so much younger than most of the guys on that team," said Brinkman, who got his first big league hit off Chester native Lew Krausse. "In fact, I'd seen many of them play when I was just a kid. Mickey was so kind and patient with me. He really helped me adjust to the big leagues.

"Mickey was laid back, not a fiery guy," Brinkman continued. "But that didn't affect how you played. As a young guy, I was going to do anything I could to play in the big leagues, and he helped me reach that goal. I would've liked to have played more years for him."

Vernon's second year in Washington got off to a staggering start. In 1962, the Senators moved into brand new DC Stadium (later to be renamed RFK Stadium), which was built at a cost of $24 million. The move made Mickey the last Senator to manage a game at Griffith Stadium and the first to do so at DC Stadium. But after winning their opener, 4-1 over Detroit with President Kennedy again throwing out the first ball and staying for the whole game, Washington lost 13 of its first 15 games. "I can't believe we're that bad," Mickey told writers.

As bad as it was on the field, the situation was rapidly deteriorating in the front office, too. In particular, Quesada's stock was plummeting rapidly.

"He had no idea what he was doing," White said. "As president of a baseball team, he was totally incompetent. He was always on Vernon's case. And his constant comments in the papers about the players infuriated them."

At one point, White quoted Vernon as saying, "What gets me most upset is that The General never tells me anything. I have to read about it in the papers." White added: "That's the angriest I ever saw Mickey get."

Noted baseball author Bill Gilbert, who had once been a Senators batboy, was the team's public relations director in 1962-63. "Quesada made all the decisions, and he was not held in very high regard as a baseball man," Gilbert said. "He thought he could order a .240 hitter to hit .280."

Several incidents during the season added to the turmoil. In one, Quesada viciously criticized several players in the press for not hustling. Woodling, a tough, no-nonsense guy, was the team's player representative. He strongly disagreed. The following day, Woodling said the team would not take the field until Quesada apologized. Vernon quelled the rebellion after calling the recalcitrant outfielder into his office for a chat.

Another time, Quesada held an all-day meeting with Vernon and others, again complaining that certain players were not hustling and that he would not tolerate such a lack of effort. "Afterward, he dictated to his secretary a press release," Gilbert recalled. "It was simply awful, but he made me hand it out in the press box. It was really embarrassing. I didn't want anything to do with it, especially since we had a lot of hustling players on the team."

As happens with all losing teams—what better example of this than the 1962 New York Mets?—there were occasional sparks of humor. Once, during an especially cold day, third base coach George Case ran into the dressing room between innings to grab a heavier shirt. Case was delayed, and before his return, the Senators had sent two batters to the plate with no third base coach.

A major storm struck during another game. After the first bolt of lightning, center fielder Willie Tasby dashed off the field. "Put [Jim] King in, I don't play in lightning," he said. Vernon had no choice but to make the substitution.

As the season continued, Washington's woes mounted. General manager Ed Doherty tried unsuccessfully to get Vernon fired. Piersall didn't hit—he would finish with a .244 batting average. Highly touted third baseman Bob Johnson was drafted for military duty, And a lack of pitching, power, catching, and a weak bench added to the dilemma.

The Piersall trade was especially frustrating. "It was a bad trade," said Vernon. "Quesada thought we needed an attraction and a center fielder. But Piersall had a bad year, and Donovan went on to have some good ones."

During the season, there were few highlights. One, however, occurred on September 12 when journeyman pitcher Tom Cheney, who had played briefly with Vernon in Pittsburgh, set a major league record by striking out 21 Boston Red Sox in a 16-inning game. The righthanded Cheney fanned 12 batters during the regulation nine innings, and struck out the side in the third, fifth, and 10th innings.

"As the game wore on, I would ask him at the start of each inning how he felt," Vernon recalled. "We didn't have pitch counts in those days, but I knew he was getting up there in pitches. He kept saying he was fine, so we kept him in. I remember he had a great curveball that day."

By the end of the season, the Senators had only one pitcher with wins in double figures—Dave Stenhouse with 11. At .310, Hinton was the only batter over .300. He and Harry Bright tied for the team lead in home runs with 17 apiece. No one else hit more than 12 homers.

"You just went out every day and did the best you could," said Hinton. "You knew you were in the big leagues, and you had to prove you belonged. And we still thought we would win every game. But it was rough. We just didn't have the personnel.

"It was a great experience for a young player like me, playing for a guy like Mickey Vernon," Hinton added. "He wasn't given many good players, but he dealt with the hand he was given. He handled it well. He did everything he could. Sometimes, though, if you don't have the horses, it doesn't matter what you do."

Vernon's horses—more accurately described as nags—wound up with a 60-101 record, one less win and one more loss than the previous year. Overmatched in virtually every respect, the Senators finished deep in last place, 10½ games behind ninth-place Kansas City, and 35½ games out of first. Washington tied for sixth in team batting average, was buried in last in runs scored, was seventh in fielding percentage, and seventh in team ERA.

The Los Angeles Angels, with a team heavily stocked with fine, young players on the way up, finished third in the American League, five games behind the second place Minnesota Twins.

After the season, Quesada fired Doherty as general manager. The job was filled by George Selkirk, a former stellar outfielder with the Yankees and at the time a scout with the Baltimore Orioles. Selkirk had been introduced to Quesada by none other than Vernon while watching an instructional league game that fall in Clearwater, Florida.

During the winter, Quesada took the peculiar step of issuing a report on the status of the team. Included in the report, that was made public through a three-part series of press releases, was a declaration of war against the media and Washington businessmen. Quesada said that the Senators were victims of a "conspiracy."

The General added to his growing reputation as a baseball anomaly by refusing to let Vernon attend the winter meetings, even though he had just given Mickey a new one-year contract. When Vernon said that he would go, even if he had to pay his own way, Quesada relented.

Even though it was hardly enough, the Senators had added more respectability to their roster in 1962. That was particularly true on the pitching staff where some good, young hurlers such as Claude Osteen, Don Rudolph, Jim Hannan, and Steve Hamilton had joined the club. By the time the 1963 season arrived, only five of the original 28 draft picks remained with the club, and it even appeared that Washington could be set to flee the American League basement.

But the wheels started to fall off almost as soon as President Kennedy threw out his third and final opening day ball. It hadn't helped that in November the club had traded Bright to the Cincinnati Reds for minor league first baseman Rogelio Alvarez (who never played a game for the Senators). But it was even worse when on April 21, Selkirk did his old team a big favor by sending the promising Hamilton to the Yankees for a highly mediocre pitcher named Jim Coates.

"We were all horrified at the deal," remembered White. "It was a terrible deal. Hamillton was very tough to hit, but he was not content as a spot starter, so I guess that's why they made the trade."

In the kind of picture you wouldn't see today, the 1963 Senators posed on the steps of the Capitol in Washington. Among those in the front row are (from left) general manager George Selkirk, George Case, Sid Hudson, Mickey Vernon, Eddie Yost, and George Susce.

Early in the season, the club's board of directors fired Quesada, replacing him with James Johnson, a banker and former World War I fighter pilot. The purge was underway. And after a 9-3 loss to the White Sox in the 40th game of the season, Vernon was informed 30 minutes before the official announcement that his services were no longer needed. The date was May 22. At the time, the club had a 14-26 record and only one player—Don Leppert—hitting above .250.

Washington players were furious. "He's one of the most decent men I've ever known," Piersall rumbled. "Vernon wasn't a player. It wasn't his fault. Maybe they should have fired us."

In making the announcement, Selkirk—who also sacked Case because of his close ties to Vernon—claimed he was "tired of mound-kicking, helmet-throwing signs of frustration. Too many of them [the players] are more concerned with their own base hits than winning games," he said. "I don't blame Mickey Vernon for the Washington Senators' status. But I fired him because of the team's place in the standings. The Senators are not a last place club."

"Houdini would have had a difficult time getting the Senators any higher in the league," responded David Condon in the Chicago *Tribune.*

In the Philadelphia *Evening Bulletin,* columnist Sandy Grady wrote, "Mickey Vernon, a genial tourist along baseball's scenic route, took the pink slip like a gentleman. That is, he didn't throw a champagne party. The Senators don't really fire managers. They give out paroles."

"In some ways, it was the humane thing to do," White said. "The Senators just weren't going anywhere. Mickey knew the game. He just had very little to work with. Yet, he was so kind to those guys. And they liked him so much. He never made them feel like they were a joke, like people made the Mets feel. The astonishing thing was that he kept them together as long as he did."

Vernon took his demise without rancor, White said. "He wasn't bitter. He didn't throw any tantrums. It's just too bad that he never had better clubs because I wonder what he would've done if he'd had more talent."

When asked more than 40 years after the firing if he was relieved, Vernon had a quick answer. "Hell, no," he said. "I was disappointed. I wanted to stay. It wasn't a bad experience. I was glad to get a chance to manage. And I wanted to manage again. I figured I was still young enough to do it."

Vernon's job as manager was filled by Gil Hodges, the former Brooklyn Dodgers first baseman and later the skipper of New York's 1969 Miracle Mets. Until the arrival of Hodges—whose contract had been acquired from the Mets in an unusual trade for a player (Piersall)—coach Eddie Yost served for one game as interim pilot.

Yost had been Vernon's long-time teammate and friend when they played together with the old Senators. After his playing days ended, he had contacted Vernon, then managing Washington, inquiring about the availability of a coaching position. Mickey hired him, and that began a 22-year coaching career that also included stints with the Mets, Red Sox, and Yankees.

"Mickey's firing disappointed me no end," Yost recalled. "He was a good friend, and he was the one who was responsible for giving me my start as a coach. I hated to see that happen to him."

He wasn't alone. "Everybody was disappointed when he was fired," said Gilbert. "From my standpoint as a PR director, he was the perfect guy to work with. I talked to him every day, and he was always 100 percent cooperative. I could call him between games of a doubleheader or at home, and he never hung up on me or told me to get the hell out of here."

"I thought he did just fine as a manager," Hudson remembered. "He didn't have much talent on that team. We were really lacking in some spots. But he was a good manager."

Vernon was offered a meaningless job as a scout. "I was going to take it," Mickey said. "But when I went up to Hal Keller's office, he gave me so much stuff to take home that I decided I didn't want the job." Having made that decision, Vernon hung around Washington for a few weeks, then headed home to Wallingford for the rest of the summer.

Meanwhile, the Senators lost nine of their first 11 games under Hodges, and by the end of the season had eclipsed the records of the two previous teams, winning only 56 games while losing 106. Again, the Nats finished in last place, this time 14½ games behind the ninth place Angels and 48½ games out of first.

CHAPTER 17

Moving Around

There are many requirements for spending a lifetime in baseball, not the least of which has to be one's willingness to live in different locations. It also helps to have a handy supply of roadmaps.

A baseball lifer, after all, goes where the jobs are. They may be in the midst of a thriving metropolis. Or they may be along a back road in the middle of nowhere. Whatever the case, the job by its very definition fosters variety. And it does not lend itself to stability.

So it was that in 1964 Mickey Vernon embarked on a new career in which he would hold jobs as a coach, manager, instructor, and scout. Over the next 24 years leading up to his retirement from baseball in 1988, he would work for eight different organizations.

Vernon's nomadic journey, moving each time to what he thought was a better job, was initiated by his removal as manager of the Washington Senators in 1963. The dismissal left Mickey without a job for the first time in his professional career.

Mickey's status among the unemployed, however, was short-lived. During the off-season, old friend Danny Murtaugh gave Vernon his former post as first base coach with the Pittsburgh Pirates.

"Danny created the job for me by sending his first base coach Ron Northey down to the minors," Vernon said. "I felt bad about that. Actually, as I look back, though, I think I still could have been playing. I think I could have played a couple more years."

As it turned out, however, Murtaugh was in the final year of his first of four terms with the Pirates. After his team finished in a tie for sixth place, the Chester native resigned because of health problems. With him went Vernon.

Like many professions, contacts made along the way can be important. And one Vernon had made as a player with the Milwaukee Braves led to his next job.

"Red Schoendienst and I had become good friends when we were with the Braves in 1959," Vernon said. "That was the year Schoendienst was having a bout with tuberculosis.

"I went to the winter meetings to look for a job, and the Los Angeles Dodgers offered me a position as a minor league hitting instructor. But then Red got the job as manager of the St. Louis Cardinals, and he asked me to join him as first base coach and hitting instructor. The Dodgers said it was okay. The only trouble with that job was that the Cardinals had won the pennant [and World Series] the year before, so once again—like Cleveland in '49 and Milwaukee in '59—I was a year too late."

Although he had deferred in Pittsburgh to Hall of Famers George Sisler and Pie Traynor, who served more or less as the Bucs' hitting coaches, Vernon had the duties as batting coach all to himself in St. Louis. "I don't show anybody how I used to hit," he said at the time. "I look for bad habits and try to correct them."

One of Vernon's most attentive students was a young left-handed pitcher who had come up from the minors at mid-season. Steve Carlton would become a Hall of Fame hurler, but he liked to hit, too. "He always came out and took batting practice early," Vernon recalled. "I would pitch to him before anybody else got there."

At Vancouver, Vernon managed the Mounties for three
seasons.

While Vernon was in St. Louis, Curt Simmons was a pitcher
with the Cardinals. "One time, he struck out Hank Aaron four
times in a row," Mickey said. "The fifth time, he threw a little
changeup and Aaron moved up in the box and hit a home run. But
he was called out for stepping out of the box."

By the following season, Vernon had relocated again. This
time he was hired by Eddie Lopat, the executive vice president of
the Kansas City Athletics, as manager of the club's Pacific Coast
League team at Vancouver. It was not only Mickey's first experience as a minor league manager, but also his first stint in the

minors since he played at Jersey City in 1940. Moreover, he knew virtually nothing about Vancouver.

Mickey wrote for a brochure on the city, checked with his old buddy George Case, who managed the Hawaii Islanders in the same league, and tried to acquaint himself with his new employer. "I'm looking forward to the job," Vernon told the author, then writing for the Delaware County *Daily Times.* "Sure, it's the minor leagues, but it's a Triple A club and it's a good opportunity."

Vernon managed in Vancouver for three seasons. His first two teams, which seldom drew more than 5,000 to a game, finished second and third in the PCL's West Division with 77-71 and 77-69 records, respectively.   After the second season, owner Charley Finley moved the Athletics to Oakland. The Mounties stayed put, but wound up in last place with a 58-88 mark. That year, the team had eight hitters bat under .250. The top home run hitter had five.

Two of the Mounties' best players while Vernon managed were Joe Rudi and Dave Duncan. But they were both called up during the season. Vernon also managed a young Sal Bando and future pilot Tony LaRussa. His only coach was pitching coach Harvey Haddix.

At the time, Greg Douglas was a young sportswriter just starting with the Vancouver *Sun.* "I was just a green, scared cub reporter, but he taught me so much," Douglas remembered. "And he was so calm. He never got ruffled. It never seemed to dawn on him how good he was.

"He not only made a great impression on me, but on the whole city," Douglas added. "He was a big part of the community. He went to booster club meetings. He met people at the ballpark. He was very popular. He was certainly one of the most respected people ever to come through Vancouver. And he's still remembered and revered."

Several memorable incidents occurred while Vernon was in Vancouver, not the least of which was one in 1967 involving a young pitcher named Roberto Rodriquez. With three weeks to go in the season, the Mounties were tied for first place while the parent Kansas City club occupied the cellar in the American League.

"We had a chance to win the pennant, but Kansas City called up Rodriquez anyway," Vernon recalled. "He didn't want to go. 'Maybe we can win the pennant,' he said. So he called Finley and told him he wasn't coming. 'Get your butt down here,' Finely told him. He joined the A's, and hardly pitched at all for them. Meanwhile, we were swept in the last three games of the season by Spokane, which won the pennant."

Another time, Jim Coates, who had come to Mickey's Senators in the ill-conceived trade for Steve Hamilton in 1963, was pitching for Seattle against the Mounties. With a 0-0 deadlock and Coates firing a no-hitter in the ninth inning, Rick Joseph was at bat for Vancouver.

"He fouled off three or four pitches, and finally Coates put one in his ribs," Vernon recalled. "Joseph charged the mound, but Coates ran toward second base. Seattle catcher Merritt Ranew tried to stop Joseph, and hit him with his mask, which later required 14 stitches. Then Ranew jumped on Joseph, and they're on the ground. I jumped on top of them. Bob Lemon was the Seattle manager, and he said, 'What the hell are you doing?' I said I was trying to get them apart.

"Well, a few innings later, Tommy Reynolds was at bat for us, and he dropped a bunt toward first base. He wanted Coates to field it so he could run over him. But Coates didn't come over, so on his way to first Reynolds veered left toward the mound. A brawl started. All hell broke loose. We had a kid named Sandy Rosario, and he hit Ranew over the head with a bat. Ranew was knocked out, and had to be flown to a hospital in Seattle. It was the worst donnybrook I ever saw.

"Later that night, Joseph went to the hotel to find Coates. Coates came out of the elevator. Nobody was around. Joseph, who had been sitting there with a hat pulled down over his face, got up and decked him."

The following day, Dewey Soriano, the president of the Pacific Coast League, flew up to meet with the principals. It turned out that Coates had hit Joseph and Reynolds the year before and there was bad blood between them. Eventually, numerous players were fined, and Rosario was suspended for the rest of the season. That winter, with Ranew and the Seattle club suing various opponents including Vernon, the case wound up in court. The suits were later dropped.

While Vernon managed in Vancouver, it was reported that the Philadelphia Phillies, then managed by his old friend Gene Mauch, were interested in Mickey's services as a coach. Mauch and Vernon had been teammates on the Boston Red Sox, and after Gene came to Philadelphia, his family sometimes stayed with the Vernons in Wallingford.

During the 1956 season, a Boston radio station had run a weekly quiz, asking players' wives five baseball questions apiece. At the end of the season, the winner was supposed to be awarded $1,000. An alligator purse was the second place prize. Lib and Mauch's wife, Nina Lee, finished in a tie for the lead and faced a runoff. But Vernon and Mauch had a special pact.

"Gene and I had lockers next to each other," Vernon recalled. "We decided they should split the money, no matter who won. Gene's wife missed all five questions, and Lib answered one of them and was actually the winner. But they had to split the money."

The job with the Phillies, however, never materialized. Neither did a coaching job in 1968 that Vernon thought he might get with the Oakland Athletics. The job fell through when A's manager Bob Kennedy was fired and replaced by Hank Bauer. "I realized when Kennedy was fired that I had no place to go in that organization," Vernon said. "So I started looking for another job. I enjoyed my three years in Vancouver. But I didn't feel they were giving me any satisfaction."

A new job arrived in the form of another managerial position, this one as skipper of the Richmond Braves, Atlanta's Triple A

As the pilot at Richmond, Mickey led a team that included leadoff batter Dusty Baker (nearest the front on bench).

farm club in the International League. Braves' general manager Paul Richards hired Mickey for the 1969 season.

Richards and Vernon had a history together, too. In 1946, when Mickey was going for the batting title, Richards was a catcher with the Detroit Tigers. Late in a game with Vernon hitless in four trips to the plate, Richards made him an offer. "I'm going to tell you what's coming," Richards said. "What kind of pitch do you want?" Vernon suggested a changeup, but when the pitch came in, he tried to bunt it, and the ball rolled foul. Richards did not make the same offer on the next pitch. As a result, Mickey failed to get a hit, and finished the game going 0-for-5.

When Vernon arrived in Richmond, he found that one of his players was none other than Sandy Rosario. Others on the team included future big leaguers Dusty Baker, Darrell Evans, and Ralph Garr. Vernon named former big league ace Virgil Trucks as his pitching coach, and the season began with much fanfare.

But Richmond, as it had done the previous year under Eddie Haas, finished in last place with a 56-83 record. For a brief time, one of Vernon's pitchers was Dick Farrell, who was released soon after giving up four straight home runs in the first inning. About the best thing that happened to Vernon all season came when he beat Buffalo Bisons manager Clyde McCullough, two pounds to four ounces, in a cow-milking contest on Dairy Night in Richmond.

The Braves, with Hal Breeden leading the league in home runs and Garr winning his second straight batting title, improved considerably in 1970, placing fifth with a 73-67 record. Richmond just missed the IL playoffs by one game.

During the season, Vernon had been criticized for not "cracking down" on his players. "That's not me," he told Jerry Lindquist in the Richmond *Times-Dispatch.* But the charge stuck, and after the season, farm director Eddie Robinson—ironically, the man for whom Vernon was traded way back in 1949—called Mickey at home and told him he was being let go. Richards, meanwhile, was quoted as saying that Vernon "had no future in the Atlanta Braves organization."

Managing was still in Vernon's blood, though, and for the 1971 season he landed a job piloting the New York Yankees' Manchester team in the Double A Eastern League. Wearing sideburns, as was the fashion of the era, Vernon appeared at a press conference, saying he wished to continue in the game as long as he could.

Clyde Klutz, the Yankees' director of player development, said that "Mickey Vernon is one of the best ever to play the game. His teaching will be his most valuable asset."

That may have been the team's only asset. The Yankees were owned at the time by Columbia Broadcasting System, and there was no desire to spend money. "It was a sorry year," Vernon said. "The Yankees were in the midst of bad times. Our uniforms must have been worn by Ruth and Gehrig. Every time some-body slid, they ripped. We had no fans. No prospects. Only one guy ever went from that team to the major leagues, and that was Matt Galante. And he went as a coach. It was just a very bad experience."

Manchester, which drew just 28,981 fans all season, went 61-75, finishing in last place in the American Division. At the end of the season, just as the expansion Senators were ending their brief 11-year stay in Washington and moving to Texas, Vernon went home to look for a new job.

He soon found it as a roving minor league hitting instructor with the Kansas City Royals. Working with the team's minor league players in spring training and in the instructional league, at the Royals' baseball academy for young Latin American players, and in the summer traveling through the farm system, Vernon spent three years with KC.

His prize pupil was future Hall of Famer George Brett, then just a teenager on the way up. "He looked like a hitter even then," Vernon recalled. "You could see he was going to be a good one. He had good hands. Made good contact."

Brett's idol was the Boston Red Sox's Carl Yastrzemski. "He tried to copy Yaz's batting style, holding his hands high," Mickey said. "You don't copy somebody else if you don't have exactly the same kinds of tools." Vernon persuaded Brett to drop his hands to a more normal position. It was good advice. Brett went on to play 17 years in the big leagues, compiling a lifetime batting average of .310.

Another person in the Royals' system with whom Vernon struck up a friendship was an up-and-coming young member of the club's minor league staff. John Schuerholz went on to become one of the top executives in baseball as the vice president and gen-eral manager of the Atlanta Braves, but in the early 1970s he was KC's assistant director of player development, and as such had regular contact with Vernon.

"Mickey was a very effective teacher," Schuerholz recalled. "He was extremely knowledgeable, and the players had a healthy respect for what he'd accomplished. He didn't try to get fancy with them, he just used basic fundamentals to try to make the guys better.

"I enjoyed every minute I had working with him," Schuerholz added. "He was as pleasant as anybody I worked with. A gentleman. Very dignified. A real professional."

After three years with the Royals, Vernon moved to the Dodgers in 1975. At the time, Dixie Walker was the club's hitting coach, but when he took a one-year sabbatical to make a trip to Ireland, Mickey joined the big club. There, with Walter Alston managing and Tom Lasorda coaching third base, Vernon was part of a distinguished staff that oversaw a starting unit that included players such as Steve Garvey, Davey Lopes, Bill Buckner, Ron Cey, and Jimmy Wynn.

One of the Dodgers' minor league players who appeared briefly for the big club that season was Phillies manager Charlie Manuel. Once a hitting coach of considerable renown himself, he played a large role in the batting success of Jim Thome while both were with the Cleveland Indians. "Mickey was a great hitting coach," Manuel said. "He really knew what he was doing. He had a great demeanor, was very well organized, and he emphasized the fundamentals of hitting. I learned quite a bit from him. "

When Walker returned the following year, Vernon was named the Dodgers' minor league hitting instructor. Then in 1977, Mickey took a job as hitting coach under manager Dick Williams with the Montreal Expos. "Looking back, I wish I'd stayed with the Dodgers," Vernon said, "because it was such a good organization."

Vernon spent two years with the Expos, devoting some of his time to the club's potentially brilliant outfield of Andre Dawson, Ellis Valentine, and Warren Cromartie.

"They were all very good outfielders with very high potential," Vernon said. "All were distinct individuals, too. Dawson was a very quiet guy with lots of ability. Valentine could have been one of the best players in the National League. He had good power, a good arm, and he ran well. But he insisted on batting with a hitch in his swing. Then he messed up his career by not taking care of himself off the field."

Vernon has a reminder of his days with the Expos. Once, while celebrities were playing softball before

In 1977, Vernon joined manager Dick Williams (right) and the Montreal Expos.

a game in Los Angeles, Cromartie and Larry Parrish got into a fight on the Montreal bench. As Vernon tried to stop it, a fist thudded heavily into his shoulder. He still carries a knot from that blow. Another time, Mickey suffered a broken nose while feeding a pitching machine. It took 10 days before the swelling receded enough for surgery to be performed. "At least one good thing came out of that incident," Vernon said. "I had broken my nose playing basketball in high school and it was always crooked after that. This straightened it out."

As an Expo, Mickey also got one of his rare ejections. He was tossed by umpire Terry Tata although he never set foot on the field. While sitting in the Montreal dugout in the midst of a game against the Chicago Cubs at Wrigley Field, he hollered an uncomplimentary observation regarding the umpire's work, and was quickly invited to leave.

After the 1978 season with Montreal, Expos general manager John McHale got a call from Yankees president and general manager Al Rosen. Vernon's friend and former rival for the 1953 batting title told McHale that he was seeking a minor league batting coach, and wanted permission to offer Mickey the job.

Rosen got permission, offered Vernon the job, and in 1979, Mickey again joined the team that for so many years when he was a player had tried to acquire him.

"One of the first players I worked with," said Vernon, "was Don Mattingly. He wanted to work on every phase of his game. He was the kind of hitter you love to see. He didn't miss many times, and rarely struck out. He almost always made good contact. The Yankees had been playing him in left field, and they had Don Demeter's son playing first base. He wasn't much good. One year they tried to make Mattingly into a second baseman in the instructional league. He could throw with either hand. Finally, they put him at first base and that's where he stayed for the rest of his career."

Vernon spent three years in the Yankees' minor league system. Along the way, he encountered another future major league executive. This time it was Doug Melvin, now the vice president and general manager of the Milwaukee Brewers, but then a minor league pitcher and, after an arm injury, a batting practice hurler with the parent club.

During the 1981 season, Lemon was hired as New York's manager. The following year he made Mickey his hitting coach, replacing the highly regarded Charlie Lau.

Mickey said that his main role would be to help players battle through slumps. "You watch them when they're going well, and you watch them when they're going bad," Vernon advised Jane Gross in the New York *Times*, "and you try to see what's causing the slump. Every once in a while, they'll get in a little rut where they get bad habits. They need work and someone to tell them what they're doing wrong. It happens to every player once in a while that they have a bad period. Some of my bad periods ran into whole years."

But after 14 games of the regular season, Lemon was dismissed. One month later, Vernon and the other coaches went, too. Replaced by Joe Pepitone, Mickey was assigned to the Yanks'

Triple A farm club at Columbus, Ohio. He remained there through the 1986 season.

Vernon served as a scout with the Yankees during the 1987 and 1988 seasons, most of the time watching National League players at Philadelphia's Veterans Stadium.

Once, however, he was sent to Minneapolis to watch a Twins player. Upon his arrival, Vernon was asked who he was scouting. "I named the player," Mickey said, "but the guy said, 'Oh, he's been traded to the Yankees.' I went all the way out there, and they never let me know."

Vernon retired after the 1988 season. He had been in professional baseball for 52 years.

The Statue and the Hall

When Mickey Vernon retired from baseball after a career that touched six decades, he ended his everyday participation in the sport. But he didn't sever his connection with the game.

Vernon made regular appearances at old-timers games. He signed autographs at baseball card shows. He was often a special guest at sports banquets, sometimes appearing at as many as three a week. And he watched baseball games of all kinds, ranging from major league to little league.

In the spring, he and a group of former major leaguers, including Early Wynn, Virgil Trucks, Hal Newhouser, Billy Klaus, Joe Ginsberg, and some others got together for one week each year in Sarasota, Florida. In 2003, at its annual mid-winter banquet, the Philadelphia Sports Writers' Association honored Vernon on the 50th anniversary of his second batting title. Mickey also played frequently in celebrity golf tournaments throughout the Philadelphia area.

For people who have been public figures, retirement can be a difficult process. It wasn't for Mickey. He remained active. And

After he retired, Vernon often appeared in old-timers games, always wearing the uniform of the Washington Senators.

appreciated. In fact, into the 21st century, Vernon was still getting five to six pieces of fan mail every day, most of them requesting his autograph.

"I feel extreme pride in the fact that wherever I go, so many people know who he is and have heard wonderful things about him," said Mickey's daughter Gay Vernon. "I'm thrilled and proud that he still receives so much fan mail. I'm proud of so many other things, too: how he has lived his life, his quiet generosity, how he worked to be the best he could be at the game, his enjoyment in instructing others how to play the game, and how he never forgot the people who helped him along the way."

Gay looks back at her life with a prominent father with warmth and passion. It is the way one would expect a person to feel who had strong family ties and grew up in a loving, healthy environment.

"When I was a youngster in elementary school," she said, "I knew my dad was a bit different than most dads. We would pack up and live in a different city every summer, and I'd even leave school in the middle of winter for six weeks in Florida or Arizona. No one else in my neighborhood did that.

"Then he was home all winter, and didn't have to go to an office like other fathers. I thought him to be special, but not really a celebrity or prominent. People did recognize him and ask for autographs, but it never got in the way of my little life. I know now that our pictures might have been in the newspaper from time to time, but I didn't know that then.

"As I got older, it was great to have him around during some of the school year. I can remember that he often was the only dad sitting in the bleachers with all the moms at my afternoon basketball games. And I loved being a baseball kid. I used to go to the ballpark early in the afternoon with my dad, and just watch batting practice and wait for the game to start. I loved the games, the traveling, making new friends every summer, and having so many wonderful adventures. To this day, whenever someone refers to a certain year or asks what I was doing at age eight, 10, or 13, it's always the summer/baseball experience I remember first."

Dating back to the 1970s, attempts had been made to name the main street in Vernon's native Marcus Hook after him. For a variety of reasons—most of them seemingly political—that never happened. Then in the 1990s, the emphasis shifted to building a statue.

It may be a true measure of a person's popularity when his peers want to erect a statute of him or her. But friends and fans of Vernon's were determined to find a way to do just that. Eventually, a group spearheaded by a number of Vernon's friends, including Chubby Imburgia and Chuck Taylor, formed a 12-person Mickey Vernon Committee to pursue the idea.

"That tells you what kind of individual he is," said former third baseman Eddie Yost, Vernon's long-time teammate in Washington. "How many times has that happened? Where else have people been willing to spend their own money to put up a statue of a guy?"

Like the naming of a street, though, the idea of a statue met with resistance, too. The ever-modest Vernon opposed the plan. And there was a battle over where to locate the statue. At least three different locations were suggested, but the committee, the boro of Marcus Hook, and others couldn't arrive at a mutually agreeable site.

"We went round and round," said Ed Gebhart, one of the leaders of the committee and the former sports editor of the Delaware County *Daily Times.* "We had talked about building a statue for years. But nobody ever did anything about it. Finally, we said, if we're going to do it, let's do it now."

Eventually, the site issue was resolved. The statue would be located on Market Street at the boro's athletic facility, one block from where Mickey grew up and the place where he played as a youth. The baseball field there would be renamed Mickey Vernon Field. The statue would be placed at the entrance.

The committee began soliciting funds. Civil engineer Chuck Catania of Milmont Park was put in charge of designing the site. Sculptor Ray Daub and Laran Bronze, a foundry in Chester, whose work is displayed all over the world, were commissioned to build a life-size statue that depicted Vernon swinging a bat. The figure would stand on a three-foot-high base.

Several hundred letters soliciting contributions were mailed. According to Gebhart, only one percent of the recipients failed to respond. And ultimately, nearly 300 individuals and companies contributed more than $60,000.

"When we started, it seemed like a very big undertaking," recalled Gebhart. "But we knew we would make it. Mickey has an awful lot of fans. Before long, the contributions started coming in, and it was just amazing. And the committee was incredible. No job was too big or too small. Everybody pitched in."

While the statue was being built, Daub measured Vernon, who originally wasn't aware of the project, from head to toe several times. Even his lips were measured. Pete Dandolos, a student at the University of Delaware with a physical stature simi-

For a number of years, former teammates such as Joe Ginsberg (left), Vernon, and Early Wynn (right) and their wives got together each spring at Sarasota, Florida.

lar to Vernon's, served as the model during the long hours of sculpting. He made 10 visits to Daub's studio, posing about three hours each time.

Ultimately, the statue was completed. The work took about nine months. At the base of the statue, along with a brief summary of Vernon's career accomplishments, were the words: "role model, mentor, great guy. A gentleman's gentleman."

Three days before the unveiling took place on September 20, 2003, U.S. Representative Curt Weldon, a Marcus Hook native and honorary chairman of the event, placed a tribute to Vernon in the Congressional Record. It said in part:

"One of the unifying bonds in our hometown is our great pride in the career and achievements of Mickey Vernon. In the ballparks of Marcus Hook, the name of Mickey Vernon is revered...Individuals like Mickey Vernon represent the essence of courage and endurance—the qualities that helped make our Nation great. He is a true American hero in every sense of the word...I ask my colleagues to join me in congratulating Mickey Vernon for his outstanding career and his major league contributions to baseball, to his community, to the Commonwealth of Pennsylvania, and to the Nation."

At about the same time, Vernon told Bob Tennant in the *Daily Times*, "I'm overwhelmed by the whole thing. When they first told me about it, they made sure to wait until the plans were well underway. They knew I'd have tried to talk them out of it. But I'm honored. And I'm thrilled."

Delaware County Council vice president Tim Murtaugh presented the distinguished native son with a resolution in which the Council declared September 20 as Mickey Vernon Day. And the testimonials began rolling in.

"Growing up on the ball fields of Marcus Hook, James Barton Vernon developed an extraordinary talent, a love of athletic competition, and a dream of turning his passion for baseball into a career," wrote Pennsylvania governor Ed Rendell. "From these humble beginnings, Mickey built a legacy that has inspired generations of young people to strive for excellence in all they do and has given a tremendous sense of pride to the community….I thank Mickey Vernon for the memories and inspiration he has given to his hometown."

Baseball commissioner Bud Selig said: "This statue stands as a fitting tribute to someone whose philosophies of hard work, sportsmanship, and teamwork have a strong bond to those developed by thousands of young adults on baseball fields across the country…Major League Baseball is truly honored to take part in this special day for Mickey."

Hall of Fame pitcher Bob Feller declared: "Mickey Vernon was the best first baseman in major league baseball for most of the years of his long career. It is fitting that his hometown of Marcus Hook dedicate a statue honoring this great American and my dear friend."

Among other testimonials:

"On top of being a great player, you are a great human being. Your career numbers are impressive. You've got me beat in everything but stolen bases and ejections." – Larry Bowa

"I congratulate those who had the foresight to establish this lasting remembrance of you. It was a pleasure to have known you as a keen and formidable, clean-cut competitor and a perfect gentleman on and off the field." – Dom DiMaggio

"You were a great hitter and a credit to baseball." – Stan Musial

"Mickey Vernon is one of the greats of the game. He and Lib are two of my favorite people. This is a great tribute to a great person and a great ballplayer." – Bill Mazeroski

"It was an honor to have played for Mickey on the expansion Senators." – Pete Burnside

The unveiling was preceded by a sold-out luncheon at Springhaven Country Club near the home in Wallingford where Mickey and Lib lived for 52 years before moving to a retirement community just outside of the town of Media. Some 230 people attended the affair. One was Chrissie Doby, daughter of the late Larry Doby, Mickey's friend going back to their days together in the Navy. Another was Sid Hudson, who had flown up with his wife from Waco, Texas. George Case Jr., was there representing his late father, as was Danny Murtaugh's son Tim, and umpire Shag Crawford.

Several hours later, the group traveled the 10 miles to Marcus Hook for the unveiling. A crowd of more than 1,000 assembled, causing the boro to block off streets near the field.

Writing in the Washington *Times*, Dick Heller captured the atmosphere: "The scene at the park was pure small-town Americana: red, white and blue bunting and flags flapping everywhere, a Dixieland combo blaring old tunes, [Harry] Kalas leading the crowd in singing *Take Me Out to the Ball Game,* and the spectators scarfing free hot dogs and Cokes. Norman Rockwell would have loved it."

Speeches and merriment were the order of the day. After all the laudatory comments, Mickey stood at the podium. "I'm so grateful...deeply moved...overwhelmed," he told the audience. "The people in Marcus Hook kept this a secret for a long time, and when they told me, they wouldn't let me talk them out of it. Baseball has

On his special day, Mickey and his daughter Gay took a close look at his statue in Marcus Hook.

given me so much. It has allowed me to see the country, experience new things, and, best of all, make so many wonderful friends."

A little while later, Vernon told Heller: "I never thought it would be anything like this. You know, when I played in Washington, all the statues around town showed men on horseback."

At the unveiling, there was, of course, another major topic of discussion involving Vernon: Mickey is a member of both the Pennsylvania and Delaware County Halls of Fame. Why isn't he in the Baseball Hall of Fame at Cooperstown?

"There's no doubt in my mind that Mickey Vernon has Hall of Fame credentials," said master of ceremonies Kalas, himself an inductee at the baseball shrine, who when he first moved to the Philadelphia area lived two blocks from Mickey in Wallingford. "Ten of the 18 first basemen in the Hall of Fame don't have as many hits as Mickey. Without question, he belongs."

Kalas has a considerable amount of company in his views. "It's time, way past time, to open the doors for a wonderful ballplayer," Heller wrote. "Veterans Committee: wake up, rise off your rumps and do your duty on behalf of Mickey Vernon."

Numerous others voiced the same sentiments in interviews for this book:

"This guy should be in the Hall of Fame. It's a shame he gets overlooked," said Yost. "One of the main reasons is that he played with the Washington Senators."

"Does Mickey Vernon belong in the Hall of Fame? You bet your boots he does," exclaimed Boston Red Sox legend Johnny Pesky. "He was a great hitter, a great fielder. I thought he was one of the best players in the American League."

"Mickey Vernon belongs in the Hall of Fame without a doubt," said former St. Louis Browns pitching standout Ned Garver, adversary of the first baseman for many years in the American League. "He measures up in every category."

"He certainly should be a candidate for the Hall of Fame," said former Senators broadcaster Bob Wolff, who first did a Washington game on TV in 1947. "He filled all of the qualifications. He could hit, hit with power, field, run, throw. What more could you want?"

"He could very well be in the Hall of Fame," added Hall of Fame second baseman Bobby Doerr of the Red Sox. "He was one of the top first basemen and a great hitter."

Sufficiently great that only 76 major league batters in the entire history of the game have more hits than Vernon, who through most of his career as a regular hit either third or fourth in the line-up and wore number 3 on his back.

An article by Jim Sargent that appeared in the August 2001 issue of *Baseball Digest* quoted former outfielder Gene Woodling, who played against Vernon and later for him on the Senators: "Mickey Vernon deserves to be in the Hall of Fame," said Woodling. "Defensively, he was the best first baseman in the league, and he was an outstanding base-runner. Mickey was one of the best all-around at first base that ever played the game."

Sargent also listed Jim Bottomley, Dan Brouthers, Orlando Cepeda, Frank Chance, Hank Greenberg, George Kelly, Harmon Killebrew, Willie McCovey, Johnny Mize, and Bill Terry as Hall of Famers who played mostly at first base and had fewer hits than Vernon. Killebrew and Tony Perez also have lower lifetime batting averages. Eight of the first basemen have fewer home runs than Vernon, five have fewer RBI, seven scored fewer runs, and 14 played in fewer games. (Numbers are based on career totals, including those games played at positions other than first base.)

The averages for Hall of Fame first basemen (Vernon's numbers in parenthesis) are: 2,034 (2,409) games, 7,491 (8,731) at-bats, 1,314 (1,196) runs, 2,332 (2,409) hits, 409 (490) doubles, 119 (120) triples, 241 (172) home runs, 1,403 (1,311) RBI, and .311 (.286) batting average. (Numbers refer only to when the player was stationed at first base.)

In a book called *The Baseball Book of Lists*, published in 1983, Dr. William Rubenstein, a college professor and member of the Society for American Baseball Research, wrote a chapter listing three teams of "old-timers who should be in the Hall of Fame but are not." The first baseman on his first team is Mickey Vernon. Gil Hodges is on the second team and Stuffy McInnis is on the third.

Another book, *All-Stars*, by Nick Acocella and Donald Dewey, listed all-time teams chosen by a number of former major league players. Nineteen of them, including Yogi Berra, George Kell, Allie

Reynolds, Mel Parnell, Don Larsen, Ferris Fain, Bob Turley, Dale Mitchell, Roy Seivers, Gene Woodling, and Al Rosen picked Vernon on their first team. Mickey received more votes than every first baseman but Lou Gehrig.

In a recent book, *Baseball's Best 1000*, by Derek Gentile, Mickey is ranked the 259th best player in major league history based on overall performance.

There is no stronger voice supporting Vernon's candidacy for the Hall than Mickey's longtime friend and former sportswriter Arthur Richman. "Without question, he should be in the Hall of Fame," said Richman. "The only reason he isn't is because he played for the Washington Senators. If he'd played for the Yankees, he would have been in the Hall 20 years ago. He was a helluva hitter, an excellent first baseman, and one of the finest gentlemen I ever met. There are people in the Hall of Fame who don't come close to James Barton Vernon."

There are many other testimonials to Vernon's credentials. His fielding records, of course, add fuel to his case. He was a member of seven All-Star teams, and was in the top 10 in the voting for Most Valuable Player three times, placing third in 1953, fifth in 1946, and ninth in 1954.

But unlike the previous format when for many years a 19-member Veterans Committee was solely responsible for electing old-timers to the Hall, a new system to send members to Cooperstown was initiated in recent years. A group of more than 100, which includes all living Hall of Fame inductees and members of the old Veterans Committee, now votes on the candidates. The new procedure makes it harder to get elected.

Vernon doesn't allow himself to be consumed by the subject. "It would be great to get elected," he said with characteristic modesty, "but I'm not spending any time worrying about it. In fact, I never think about it unless somebody brings it up. "

And yet, as columnist Jack McCaffery wrote in the Delaware County *Daily Times*, "his defense, his hitting, his decency were of Hall of Fame caliber."

Vernon is often asked to name an all-star team consisting of players he saw during his 52 years in baseball. Ted Williams in left field, Joe DiMaggio by a slim margin over Willie Mays in center, Mike Schmidt at third base, Bob Feller as a righthanded pitcher, and Warren Spahn as a lefty are certain choices for him. The other positions have too many candidates to narrow down to one each.

Mickey names Hank Aaron, Roberto Clemente, and Al Kaline in right field, Lou Gehrig, Jimmie Foxx, and Stan Musial at first base; Charley Gehringer, Joe Morgan, Joe Gordon, Bobby Doerr, Bill Mazeroski, and Jackie Robinson at second; Ernie Banks, Luke Appling, Pee Wee Reese, Lou Boudreau, Ozzie Smith, Luis Aparacio, and Larry Bowa at shortstop; and Bill Dickey, Mickey Cochrane, Roy Campanella, Yogi Berra, and Johnny Bench at catcher.

Vernon rates the 1949-53 New York Yankees as the greatest team he's ever seen.

In 2005, after the Montreal Expos had relocated to Washington, new attention was directed toward Mickey and other former Senators. And when the new Nationals opened the season, their first series was played against the Phillies in Philadelphia. As both a member of the original and the expansion Washington Senators and a native of the Philadelphia area, Vernon was chosen to throw out the ceremonial first pitch in the second game.

When that night arrived, Vernon's strong toss from the mound at Citizens Bank Park highlighted a banner evening that also included an assortment of newspaper, radio, and television interviews, the presence of four busloads of fans from Delaware County, the chance to see old friends such as Charlie Manuel, Frank Robinson, and Milt Thompson, and the red-carpet treatment by the Phillies, including dinner in the executive dining room. For one night again, Mickey, accompanied to the event by Gay, her husband John Brande, and sister Edith Cushman, was the center of attention.

It was an appropriate way to recognize a man who not only had a storied career in baseball, but who was the consummate professional and one of the classiest gentlemen ever to play the game.

CHAPTER 19

For the Record

Career Batting and Fielding Records

Year	Team	G	BA	AB	H	2B	3B	HR	R	RBI	PO	A	E	Pct.
1937	Easton	83	.287	300	51	24	6	10	86	64	814	54	**16**	.982
1938	Greenville	132	.328	524	172	31	12	1	84	72	1159	74	*24*	.981
1939	Springfield	69	.343	268	92	13	7	3	52	41	601	31	6	991
1939	Washington	76	.257	276	71	15	4	1	23	30	690	40	11	.985
1940	Jersey City	154	.283	569	161	2	9	9	76	65	1305	75	16	.989
1940	Washington	5	.158	19	3	0	0	0	0	0	41	2	0	1.000
1941	Washington	138	.299	531	159	27	11	9	73	93	1186	80	10	.992
1942	Washington	151	.271	621	168	34	6	9	76	86	1360	95	**26**	.982
1943	Washington	145	.268	553	148	29	8	7	89	70	1351	75	14	.990
1944-45	In military service													
1946	Washington	148	**.353**	587	207	**51**	8	8	88	85	1320	101	*15*	.990
1947	Washington	154	.265	600	159	29	12	7	77	85	1299	105	*19*	.987
1948	Washington	150	.242	558	135	27	7	3	78	48	1297	113	15	.989
1949	Cleveland	153	.291	584	170	27	4	18	72	83	**1438**	**155**	14	.991
1950	Clev-Wash	118	.281	417	117	17	3	9	55	75	959	78	9	*.991*
1951	Washington	141	.293	546	160	30	7	9	69	87	1157	87	8	**.994**
1952	Washington	154	.251	569	143	33	9	10	71	80	1291	115	10	**.993**
1953	Washington	152	**.337**	608	205	**43**	11	15	101	115	**1376**	94	12	.992
1954	Washington	151	.290	597	173	**33**	14	20	90	97	**1365**	76	11	**.992**
1955	Washington	150	.301	538	162	23	8	14	74	85	1258	69	8	.994
1956	Boston	119	.310	403	125	28	4	15	67	84	930	58	11	.989
1957	Boston	102	.241	270	65	18	1	7	36	38	662	51	6	.992
1958	Cleveland	119	.293	355	104	22	3	8	49	55	774	50	11	.987
1959	Milwaukee	74	.220	91	20	4	0	3	7	20	65	4	2	.972
1960	Pittsburgh	9	.125	8	1	0	0	0	0	1	0	0	0	–
Major League totals		2409	.286	8731	2495	490	120	172	1196	1311	19819	1448	212	.990
All-Star Game totals		7	.143	14	2	0	0	0	2	1	21	1	0	1.000

Bold – led league.
Italic – tied for league lead

All-Time Records for First Basemen

Major league record – most double plays, career – 2,044
American League records–most games played, career – 2,227; most chances, career – 21,198; most putouts, career – 19,754; most assists career, 1,444; most double plays, career — 2,041.

Grand Slam Home Runs*

Date	Opponents	Inning	Pitcher
August 12, 1955	Washington at Boston	Seventh	Tom Hurd
April 25, 1958	Detroit at Cleveland	Third	Jim Bunning

Inside the Park Home Runs*

Date	Opponents	Inning	Pitcher
August 15, 1943	Washington at Cleveland	Seventh	Allie Reynolds
June 1, 1946	Detroit at Washington	Eighth	Fred Hutchinson
July 28, 1946	Washington at Cleveland	First	Allie Reynolds
September 20, 1952	Boston at Washington	Fourth	Willard Nixon

Pinch Hit Home Runs*

Date	Opponents	Inning	Pitcher
May 2, 1959	San Francisco at Milwaukee	Ninth	Stu Miller
August 22, 1959	Chicago at Milwaukee	Seventh	Dave Hillman

Hitting for the Cycle*

Date	Opponents	Inning	Pitcher
May 19, 1946	Washington at Chicago		Eddie Lopat

*Source: Tattersall-McConnell Home Run Log, Society for American Baseball Research

Triple Plays

As a Fielder:

September 14, 1941   Detroit at Washington   Second Inning

Batter Pinky Higgins, Bruce Campbell on first, Rudy York on second.

Higgins lines out to Mickey Vernon at first. Vernon steps on base to retire Campbell, throws to shortstop Cecil Travis at second to retire York (3-6).

May 22, 1952   New York at Washington   Ninth Inning

Batter Irv Noren, Art Schult at first, Andy Carey at second.

Noren lines out to pitcher Bob Porterfield, who throws to Mickey Vernon at first to retire Schult. Vernon throws to shortstop Pete Runnels at second to retire Carey (1-3-6).

As a Base-runner:

September 19, 1939   Cleveland at Washington   Fifth Inning

Batter Early Wynn, Al Evans at first, Mickey Vernon at second.

Wynn grounds to third baseman Ken Keltner, who throws to shortstop Lou Boudreau at second to retire Vernon. Boudreau throws to Oscar Grimes at first, who tags out Evans and retires Wynn at the base. (5-6-3).

September 25, 1946   Washington at Philadelphia   Seventh Inning

Batter Cecil Travis, Stan Spence at first, Mickey Vernon at third.

Travis grounds to third baseman Don Richmond, who throws to second baseman Oscar Grimes to retire Spence at second. Vernon caught in rundown with throws going from Grimes to Richmond to catcher Joe Astroth to Richmond to Astroth to Richmond, who tags out Vernon. Richmond throws to shortstop Jack Wallaesa at second to retire Travis (5-4-5-2-5-2-5-6).

As a Batter:

September 22, 1954   Washington at New York   Sixth Inning

Batter Mickey Vernon, Pete Runnels at first, Wayne Terwilliger at second.

Vernon lines out to Bill Skowron at first. Skowron steps on first to retire Runnels, throws to shortstop Jerry Coleman at second to retire Terwilliger (3-6)

Source: Triple Play Database assembled by Herm Krabbenhoft,
   Jim Smith, and Steve Boren.

Transactions

December 14, 1948 – Washington Senators trade Mickey Vernon and pitcher Early Wynn to Cleveland Indians for pitchers Ed Klieman and Joe Haynes, and first baseman Eddie Robinson.

June 14, 1950 – Cleveland Indians trade Mickey Vernon to Washington Senators for pitcher Dick Weik.

November 8, 1955 – Washington Senators trade Mickey Vernon, pitchers Bob Porterfield and Johnny Schmitz, and outfielder Tom Umphlett to Boston Red Sox for pitchers Dick Brodowski, Tex Clevenger, and Al Curtis, and outfielders Karl Olson and Neil Chrisley.

January 29, 1958 – Boston Red Sox sell Mickey Vernon to Cleveland Indians.

April 11, 1959 – Cleveland Indians trade Mickey Vernon to Milwaukee Braves for pitcher Humberto Robinson.

October 13, 1959 – Milwaukee Braves give Mickey Vernon his unconditional release.

Special Honors

All-Star Game selections: 1946, 1948, 1953, 1954, 1955, 1956, 1958.
Most Valuable Player Award finishes: 1946 (fifth), 1953 (third), 1954 (ninth)

Coaching

1960, 1964 - Pittsburgh Pirates, first base coach
1965 - St. Louis Cardinals, batting coach
1972-74 - Kansas City Royals, minor league hitting instructor
1975 - Los Angeles Dodgers, batting coach
1976 - Los Angeles Dodgers, minor league hitting instructor
1977-78 - Montreal Expos, batting coach
1979-81, 1982-86 - New York Yankees minor league hitting instructor
1982 - New York Yankees, batting coach

Records as a Manager

Year	Team	League	Games	Won	Lost	Tie	Pct.	Finish
1961	Washington	American	161	61	100	0	.379	9(T)
1962	Washington	American	162	60	101	1	.373	10
1963	Washington	American	40	14	26	0	.350	–
1966	Vancouver	Pacific Coast	148	77	71	0	.520	2 (W)
1967	Vancouver	Pacific Coast	146	77	69	0	.527	3 (W)
1968	Vancouver	Pacific Coast	146	58	88	0	.397	6 (W)
1969	Richmond	International	139	56	83	0	.403	8
1970	Richmond	International	140	73	67	0	.521	5
1971	Manchester	Eastern	136	61	75	0	.449	4 (A)
Major League record			363	135	227	1	.373	
Minor League record			855	402	453	0	.470	

Photo Credits

Photos from the collection of Mickey Vernon, pages 14, 23, 42, 43, 50, 57, 61, 64, 70, 73, 75, 76, 83, 84, 86, 89, 94, 97, 101, 106, 110, 113, 119, 127, 133, 135, 136, 140, 142, 143, 146, 152, 154, 160, 167, 174, 176, 186, 193, 197, 201, 206, 209

Urban Archives, Temple University, Philadelphia, pages 9, 125, 163

National Baseball Hall of Fame Library, Cooperstown, New York, pages 26, 54, 129, 179, 217

Delaware County *Daily Times*, photo by Eric Hartline, page 212

Photos courtesy of the Philadelphia Athletics Historical Society, pages 33, 68, 181

Photos courtesy of Gay Vernon, pages 3, 37, 156